Port Out, Starboard Home

the rise and fall of the ocean passage

Anna Sproule

BLANDFORD PRESS
Poole · Dorset

By the same author

The Social Calendar

Cover/Jacket: The Galley of HMS Calcutta (Portsmouth) by Tissot, Tate Gallery, London

Endpapers: departure of P & O steamer *Sumatra* from Southampton for India, 10 April 1875

Produced by MIDAS BOOKS

First published 1978 by
BLANDFORD PRESS LTD.,
Link House, West Street,
Poole, Dorset, BH15 1LL

Designed by Brian Jewell

ISBN 0 7137 8522 5

Printed in Scotland
by John G Eccles Printers Ltd, Inverness

Contents

1. *Port Outward — Starboard Home*

In early December 1915, three letters arrived in quick succession in the remote Northamptonshire village of Sudborough. The envelopes were the regulation green of the Forces mail and bore the equally regulation testimony of the writer that, on his honour, the contents 'referred to nothing but private and family matters'. The contents themselves — pencil-written on narrow sheets of scrap paper — described the various hazards of a passage to India in war.

Or perhaps it was not India after all. The writer, an Indian Army major of the conscientious and worrying sort, confessed that he was by no means sure. His orders were to re-join his regiment, but he was in 'utter ignorance' as to where it had gone during the three weeks' leave he had spent in England. However, he said, he had the feeling that most of it was by now in Egypt; he would get further information when he got there.

He had left Marseilles on board P & O's S.S. *Egra* on 22 November, taking with him his camp kit (which had arrived on board well after he had), his new spectacles, the Brilliantine and the medicine for his lumbago that he had bought in London, and a biography of the Duke of Marlborough, but lamenting the lack of his solar topi. It was being sent to him by post and had missed the boat. However, he wrote in the first of those three letters to his wife, the weather was still quite cool. He went on:

'We have a lot of gunners aboard, and two guns mounted over the stern to give submarines a warm reception. So far none have appeared. We come a very long course nowadays round the north of Corsica, as the Straits of Bonifacio are closed, then south of Sicily until we hit the African coast near Derna. I sit at the captain's table; the captain is a nice little man and an even bigger fresh-air fiend than I am .... On one thing you can make up your mind: you will not take an ocean voyage (to India) until the submarines have been cleared out of the Mediterranean. I don't think it's good enough for women and children to take the risk unless they have to. So settle down at Sudborough until the spring at any rate.

The second letter was much shorter. Dated 28 November, it urged his wife to send £10 to his account at the Army & Navy Stores, Bombay, so that he could buy toothpaste and shaving soap on arrival, and added that he'd had a 'bad experience' at Alexandria.

Opposite: deck scene on P & O's *Himalaya*, 1853.

The third letter, written the next day and posted in a flourish of Arabic franking-marks in Port Taufic, explained what had happened. He had been left behind. At Alexandria, the *Egra*'s skipper announced that there were 900-odd bags of mail to unload and departure for Port Said and the Suez Canal would not take place until the morning. Among the passengers, there was a general rush for the shore, and against his better judgment — 'I had nothing to do there, and we were lying a long way out' — the letter-writer found himself swept up in the throng.

We got into the quay in 15 minutes, so told the steam-launch to be ready at 6.30 to get us back to the ship by seven in time for dinner. After a walk and a drink, we got back to the quay at 6.15, and collected eight officers and four NCO's by 6.30, but there was no launch. We decided to hire a sailing boat, and started off.

To make the story short, we cruised about in that infernal harbour for three hours without finding the *Egra*. It is, of course, a very big harbour, very full of shipping, and it was a dark night. When at sea, all (troop) transports travel with all lights screened, and there were nothing but riding lights to steer by. We boarded two or three vessels to get information, and hailed a lot more, and all except one said the *Egra* was 'over there, all right'. One man said he wasn't sure but he rather thought he'd seen the *Egra* just outside the harbour at dusk; we all agreed he was a liar.

At last, we made for the nearest wharf and there, after much searching, found the naval transport officer who told us the *Egra* had gone; he advised us to go to the staff officer concerned and gave us his address. We packed into three gharries and drove off. He was in bed and asleep — it was now 11 pm — but we had him out, and he said we must follow by train to Port Said as (the ship's) orders were to go right through at once. There was a very slow and bad train going at 11.30 pm, reaching Port Said at 12 noon, with a change and halt at Benha from 4 am to 8 am, whereas there was another good train leaving at 9 am the next day and due at 3.30. He wouldn't hear of us waiting till next morning, so we just got to the station in time to catch the train. We hadn't a greatcoat between us, no dinner, and could only just pay the fares by collecting all we had among us. You can imagine the night: four in a carriage and not even a rug or a pillow. Turned out at four in the morning, and made tracks for the buffet, which was closed. The man lived in the town three miles off, but, thank goodness, we were back in the land of bakshish, and a young villain ran off to call him. By 7 am he had a good *chota hazri* (breakfast) ready, and we got our aching voids pacified, if not filled. The eggs gave out, of course, before we had had half enough. At 8 am we boarded the Cairo-Port Said express and our troubles were over. We found a young staff officer waiting to meet us with orders to take us on board, so we crept onto the ship feeling very silly . . . .

Despite himself, and very much by accident, the present writer's grandfather had made a personal re-discovery of part of one of the most ancient travel routes in the world. The details of his scrambled journey — the resourcefulness, the cavalier attitude to the local population, the British Raj jargon, the waiting place at the captain's table, accorded to the highest-ranking officers aboard, even the unwanted solar topi lost in the post — are as redolent of the early twentieth century as *Greenmantle* and the *Thirty-Nine Steps*; the Overland Route which, from Alexandria to the Nile, he followed dates back to the beginning of

Overland with P & O: a rest house for passengers crossing the Egyptian desert between Cairo and Suez in the pre-Canal period.

history. Long before the Vikings started to entrust themselves, their families and their livestock to the open boats in which they sailed across the Atlantic to Greenland, and even before the Romans' military and naval genius had brought most of Europe within the limits of the 'known' world, the shipmasters of the East had developed a unique land-and-sea approach to the business of getting their cargoes of spice and precious stones to the emerging civilisations in and around the Mediterranean. Picking their season for travel, they sailed with the help of the favouring monsoon to the Egyptian coast of the Red Sea; loaded their wares onto donkeys and camels to make the desert crossing from the sea to the Nile; re-loaded them on to river boats and progressed down the Nile to the other sea. In the earliest times, indeed, they had even had man-made waterways to help them: the ancient Egyptians, and the Assyrians who conquered them, constructed a series of canals from the Red Sea to the Nile. When these — contemporary reports of which gave Ferdinand de Lesseps the inspiration for the construction of today's Suez Canal — finally got silted up, the East-West traders switched to the camel-train procedure for good.

By the Middle Ages, their route had earned a name for itself: the Pepper Road. Until the early Renaissance, when developments in European navigation skills joined with an increased demand for trading outlets and quick profits to send three-masted, castle-bowed caravels out in all directions over the Atlantic, the Western world relied for its luxury goods, drugs and spices on a trade link that had been established in the time of the Pharoahs. That it had manifold disadvantages went without saying: the worst was that the Mediterranean could be — and, in the sixteenth century, was — easily controlled by Europe's chief public enemies, the Muslim peoples of the Near East. So, when the caravels found their way down Africa to the Cape of Good Hope

Camel train on the Overland Route between the Mediterranean and the Red Sea.

and then north-eastwards towards India, the merchants and customers of Europe cheerfully settled for a trading route that, however long and perilous, was free from political interference. The Pepper Road, though never entirely superseded, had been decisively supplemented, and the world's major shipping initiatives had passed from the East to the maritime nations of the Atlantic, where they would remain until the twentieth century. The quest for the Spice Islands and Cathay might lead men to unexpected destinations, unprecedented dangers, and even death; but their efforts, unlike those of the Greenland-bound Vikings of the tenth century, established once and for all that a long-distance, truly intercontinental ocean passage was a practical proposition.

It was not, however, one that immediately recommended itself to any but a small group of professional pioneers: seamen, traders, diplomats. Although the average well-to-do European travelled for both business and pleasure surprisingly frequently, his seafarings were confined to the Atlantic coast, the North Sea or the tideless Mediterranean. Journey times — thirty days, for example, from Venice to Crete in summer, a possible sixty in winter — ensured that he would have plenty of time for contemplating the queasy wretchedness of his position and for resolving to repeat the experience as seldom as possible in the future. For him and his contemporaries, therefore, sea journeys were dismal enough even in the best of circumstances; to venture into what was then the all-but-unknown was pointless folly. The world's great ocean shipping routes — the north and south Atlantic runs, the passage round the Cape of Good Hope to India, Australia and the Far East, the return journey via Cape Horn — were developed, not for the benefit of passengers, but according to the almost invariable formula of exploration/trade/conquest/settlement. The first ocean travellers to use these routes in any quantity fell into the two melancholy categories of slaves and soldiers. The slaves, travelling from Africa under conditions of repulsive cruelty, went to the newly-established plantations in the New World; the soldiers sailed to wherever indigenous populations appeared likely to offer resistance to Europe's take-over bid. Only when the trading station or military presence became established enough to demand the services of — or protect — auxiliaries such as administrators, farmers, craftsmen, clerks, and engineers did the voluntary ocean traveller begin to emerge, followed (as the settlement grew progressively more settled) by his wife.

The names of the world's main coastal cities, listed at the time of the Napoleonic wars, show both the results of the enterprise demonstrated by this new type of long-distance seafarer and also his country of origin. Boston, New York (formerly New Amsterdam), San Francisco; Rio de Janeiro, Montevideo, Santiago; Cape Town; Melbourne, Sydney . . . . Only India and the Far East, backed by centuries of tradition, had managed to avoid the spatter of European-inspired place-names that was appearing across the world's continents. All the same, the scale of travel between these outposts of Western civilisation and their heartland was still dimunitive compared with today's. It could hardly be otherwise: few had the time, money or inclination to embark on a four-to-six-month voyage to India or on the

On a Nile steamer to Cairo.

Homeward bound in the 1860s: a British ship leaves Sandridge Railway Pier, Australia.

even longer one to the Far East (a round trip to China took two to three *years*), while most of the passengers to Australia were convicts.

The North Atlantic, true, was different: the peasant farmers of Ireland and Scotland (the latter dispossessed by the Highland Clearances) had, by force of stark necessity, taken the lead in a migratory movement that would in fifty years become a flood. They travelled in conditions of chaotic squalor; in the view of Basil Greenhill, director of the National Maritime Museum at Greenwich, the empty cargo space in which they were accommodated offered quarters 'little different from those in which the Pilgrim Fathers had travelled'. The *Mayflower*, which had sailed in 1620, had offered an area of deck 'less than the area of a small sofa' to each passenger. The Atlantic merchant ships of the eighteenth century, which carried loads of timber and flax to Europe and filled up with a human cargo at bargain passage rates for what would otherwise have been an unprofitable westward run, allotted emigrants a bunk berth eighteen inches wide, with two foot of headroom.

The journey lasted anything up to sixty days, and the fact that any embarked at all on an ordeal of such magnitude was a measure of their desperation. But, for all that they formed the biggest passenger group of their day, their numbers were minute compared with what was to come.

At the end of the eighteenth century, the annual total of long-distance ocean travellers could still be counted in thousands; by the end of the nineteenth, totals would be in the million bracket. Almost within the space of a single lifetime, sea travel had come of age. Something that for thousands of years had been the specialised affair of the professional, the adventurer, and — as in the case of both convicts and emigrants — the outcast, quite suddenly turned into an element of ordinary life, as lived by quite ordinary people.

The change was one of stupendous proportions — but, inevitably, it is almost impossible to pinpoint the year when it started. As the following chapters will show, 1816 marked the beginning in one sense, 1819 in another. The 1830s, however, probably represent the crucial period, and from then on scarcely a year went by without something happening to help to boost the passenger shipping world to the heights it would occupy by the time the century closed. It might be a change in world economics, or a sudden explosion of national pride, or — as in the case of Ireland — a disastrous crop failure. It was frequently a case of making spectacular acquiescence to ever-rising consumer standards: if passengers, or the big spenders among them, wanted faster journey times, heating in the cabins, more lavatories, and grand pianos, the laws of good business practice ensured that they got them as soon as the mechanical problems involved had been mastered. There were the initiatives — often, it must be said, tardy ones — of naval authorities and Postmasters General: one of the greatest incentives for breaking speed records on the high seas was the cash reward for carrying mail as fast as possible from one place to another. Above all, there were the technological advances — advances which, in chicken-and-egg fashion, were created by the strength of passenger demand and created further demand in their turn.

The chief of these, of course, was the introduction of the steamship. After a cut-throat, and astonishingly prolonged, battle with its rival, sail, steam and its concomitant advantages of vastly increased speed, tonnage and reliability succeeded in transforming the world of ocean travel. In fact, it transformed the world itself. Communication between one continent and another could now be achieved within weeks rather than months, days rather than weeks. The transport of huge numbers of people — engaged in peaceful purposes or, more disturbingly, military ones — became possible. The world over, existing cities grew and new ones sprang up to service the great ships that called at them. The shipping companies themselves — Cunard and White Star on the

Canal excavations get under way in Egypt.

North Atlantic, Canadian Pacific with its *Empresses* on both Atlantic and Pacific, Royal Mail on the South Atlantic, Union-Castle and Elder Dempster for the African run, Shaw Savill for New Zealand — became household names, while one of their number was directly involved in events leading to the literal separation of the African continent from Asia. It is ironic that the building of the Suez Canal nearly ruined the firm which had done so much to create the demand for it and which in the future it would so markedly benefit: the Peninsular and Oriental Steam Navigation Company.

The P & O: the two initials are among the most evocative business names in the world. Cane-backed chairs; dashing cavalry officers; curry and tiffin and whisky livers; velvet nights in the tropics; Bombay's Taj Hotel and the 'Gateway of India'; ship's concerts, and bridge, and bright-eyed girls journeying to find husbands in Poona — it all adds up to a glorious dream of the Empire as it wasn't. Reality, while it included these elements, also meant a sad Europe-bound stream of child passengers, facing years of separation from their parents on health and educational grounds. It meant frenzied last-minute checks of home medicine kits, the most important items in which were quinine for malaria and morphine for up-country emergencies when the nearest doctor was three days' travel away. It meant temperatures that brought a new word into the English language: 'posh' derives from 'Port Outward — Starboard Homeward', which was the shorthand description of the accommodation accorded to VIPs travelling through the Red Sea. The point was that, on the outward journey, cabins on the ship's port (eastward-facing) side escaped the daily afternoon sun-roasting and so were much cooler to sleep in than their starboard twins. Going back, the situation was reversed.

Heat, languour, seasickness; the dust of the coaling ports; the unwelcome attentions of dockside vendors of ostrich feathers, curios, cigarettes, postcards; hearty meals which few felt like eating (an early P & O menu features sucking pigs, braised sheep's head and pancakes as well as curry) — these were the true hallmarks of a passage east in the days of Imperial pomp. And passengers travelling with P & O before 1869, when the Suez Canal was opened, had further complications to deal with. From Alexandria to Suez, they went overland by the old Pepper Road.

The history of P & O, with its mixture of luck, commercial courage, persistence, vision and canny accounting, is in many ways a typical example of how the world's great shipping lines of the nineteenth century came to be formed. Starting in 1837, with a handful of paddle-steamers running between London and Gibraltar, and backed by a vital government mail contract, the Peninsular Steam Navigation Company speedily set its sights higher, was re-launched as the Peninsular and Oriental, and extended its services to take in Egypt, India, the Far East and, eventually, Australia. What makes the company unique, however, is the way it reached back to the beginning of history for the key to its success. The Overland Route — horse-drawn

The Empress Eugenie of France rides a camel to the opening of the Suez Canal, 1869.

Canal section of the Overland Route.

canal boat from Alexandria to the Nile, Arab sailing craft up the Nile to Cairo, donkeys and camels across the desert to Suez — was still used, though seldom by Europeans, and it offered a much quicker method of getting to India than the passage round Africa. The only trouble was that it was indescribably uncomfortable.

Hardy travellers were recommended to take both their own food and their own water; they were also exhorted to have their conveyance on the Nile scuttled and sunk for two or three days before embarking, as this was the only way of killing all the bugs that lived on it. In addition, there was plague in the area, and both Italy and France insisted on Europe-bound travellers from Egypt spending a period in quarantine. P & O set to work, providing its own vessels for the river and canal stages, enlarged and beautified the rest-houses along the way, and, for the desert crossing, laid on carriages whose drivers made a point of trying to race each other. (Goods, coal and spare parts for the Suez-India ships, however, went the whole way on camel-back.) As improved, the crossing of the Overland Route took just over three days, part of which was allowed off for rest, refreshment and the inspection of historical monuments.

Things were improved still further when the Pasha of Egypt, with P & O's moral and financial backing, built a railway from Alexandria to Cairo and beyond. P & O was delighted, and so at first was its steadily-increasing passenger-roll. But the delight did not last long, as is shown by the account of one John Beames, a member of the 'Indian Civil' in the pay of the East India Company. John went out to India by P & O in 1858; apart from seasickness in the Bay of Biscay ('I lay sick unto death as it seemed'), his voyage was pleasant enough until Egypt and after Suez, but remarkably uncomfortable in between. He wrote in his memoirs:

> We left Cairo early in the morning by train but, after an hour's journey, the railway suddenly left off in the middle of the desert. Our baggage was put on camels led by Abraham, Isaac and Jacob living in the flesh, and the passengers were closely packed into small green omnibuses on two wheels drawn by mules, six of us in each. There was a long procession of them and they plunged and jolted most uncomfortably. We reached dirty Suez as the sun was setting and after a wretched fly-haunted meal in the bare caravanserai of an hotel, went on board the *Bengal*, a large roomy old tub of a vessel long since broken up.

Clearly, further improvements still were needed. But, when they came in the definitive shape of the French-, Turkish- and Egypt-backed Suez Canal, the event nearly put P & O out of business. In the end, though, the company managed to cut its Overland Route losses, secure new mail contracts, build ships suited to the new through journey, and use the canal with the best of them.

The story of passenger shipping in the east, in which P & O continued to play a key role, had come full circle. The Overland Route might — except for the tourists and those who had missed their boat

The Suez Canal opens to traffic.

— have vanished for ever, but the projects of Pharaohs had been triumphantly re-created. What, however, about the west?

Here, too, the steamship would cut a huge land-mass in two: the Panama Canal, officially opened in 1920, was actually in use by the end of 1914. But this is only one episode in a history that, while paralleling that of P & O, is written on a much grander scale. It was the countries of the west that brought shipping out of its Dark Ages and turned it into what we know today — and it was on the ocean that fringed them that they made their early experiments, put their later discoveries into practice and experienced their worst disasters and most far-reaching successes. It was on the North Atlantic that steam made its ocean debut; it was there that the strategies and rules governing the profitable shipping of human cargo were worked out; it was there that the majority of the steamships successively hailed in their time as the world's biggest and best were put to work. The eastern routes, with their complications of the canal, the heat and the huge distances involved, formed a specialised sub-section — though a very large one — of the passenger shipping business; the Atlantic was its birthplace, its breeding-ground for new trends, its basic bread-and-butter. Just how the birth took place, how the trends multiplied and how the butter was soon supplemented with jam forms the main story of this book.

2. *The Great Race*

On June 17 1819, a look-out stationed at Ireland's southernmost point, Cape Clear, noticed a three-masted square-rigged ship coming up fast from the open Atlantic — and, in spite of the headway it was making, it seemed to be on fire. It was belching smoke and sparks in an unmistakable fashion, and all its sails were gone. He rushed off a message to the nearby naval authorities, who instantly sent HM Revenue cutter *Kite* off on a dramatic mercy dash.

It is hard to see what else the look-out could have done. He was not to know that the drama would swiftly change into wildest farce; that his prompt action would result in red-faced immortality for both himself and the rescue ship; that he was witnessing an event that would totally transform the whole business of an ocean passage.

What he had seen was not a ship in the process of burning to the water-line but the arrival in British waters of the paddle-steamer *Savannah*, bound for Liverpool, Stockholm and Russia and the first vessel to have crossed an ocean with the help of steam. With the help only; *Savannah* had sailed most of the way. Her collapsible side paddles had churned her along for no more than eighty-five of the 700-plus hours of the voyage. She guzzled coal; at the start of her voyage from New York to Liverpool, her bunkers were so full of coal and wood that she sat too low in the water for the paddles to function. By the time she sighted Cape Clear, most of it had gone. 'No cole', the log-book was to note the next day, 'to git up steam.'

The *Savannah* was, all the same, nowhere near in need of rescue. Ignoring the *Kite* spanking up to her aid, she paddled grimly on and outdistanced her would-be helpers. The *Kite* proceeded to compound its future embarrassment by letting off a few cautionary shots in the *Savannah*'s direction. Better to be boarded than blown up: the *Savannah* gave in, stopped and welcomed the *Kite*'s officers aboard.

The little steamer-cum-sailor finally docked outside the Liverpool bar on the evening of 20 June. She had taken twenty-nine days and a half to make the crossing, by no means a record time even in those days. The average eastbound time taken by an ordinary packet-ship was

Compass card of the 1820s.

twenty-three days — the westbound trip 'against the wind' took much longer — and one of them, the flying *Canada*, did it in just over a fortnight. The *Savannah* was visited by scores of Liverpudlians in small boats and later inspected with interest by the King of Sweden and the Lord High Admiral of Russia. (Her promoters hoped to sell her to the Czar.) She was certainly a curiosity; but at that time no one felt in the mood to take things further. Some, indeed, believed that she was the next best thing to the devil's work; the crossing, said one Jeremiah, was the 'most dangerous thing' that had taken place in the history of shipping. Unregarded and unsold, the ship that had done it chugged and lolloped her way home again, was offered to the United States Navy and refused, had her engines taken out, made nine trips as a sailing packet up and down the eastern American seaboard, and, in 1821, finally ran aground on Long Island and broke up. And that, as far as the general public was concerned, seemed to be that. No paying passenger had yet crossed the Atlantic under steam power; the *Savannah*, rather pathetically, had been provided with mirrors, oriental carpets and state rooms, but no one had been persuaded to take advantage of these amenities. For nearly a decade afterwards, it looked as if no one would.

In pre-Victorian maritime circles — Princess Victoria, later to become Queen, had in fact been born on the day that the *Savannah* put to sea from New York — steam was still regarded very much as it had been when the Greek mathematician Hero had demonstrated its possibilities to his fellow Alexandrians 2000 years before. He developed a gadget that, to modern eyes, looks like a lavatory ballcock mounted on a pressure-cooker; when the water in the 'cooker' was heated, it turned into steam, expanded into the ballcock's hollow mountings and forced its way out through right-angled spouts let into the ballcock itself. The ball revolved 'after the fashion of dancing figures'. Very interesting, Hero's contemporaries had said — but what was the point? In a slave economy, of course, there *was* no point; automation was a non-starter. It was true that, by the early nineteenth century, steam-power was already in use for mine-pumping and haulage, and the earliest primitive steam locomotives had been built; but as far as sea transport was concerned there was no evident reason to replace the traditional source of power: the wind, caught in skilfully-fashioned canvas and commanded by cheap seafaring labour. Small paddle-boats were already plying their trade in European coastal waters, on the large American rivers such as the Mississippi, and on the Neva in Russia (it was this one, called the *Elizabeth*, that the *Savannah* aimed to rival). But the Atlantic passage, to say nothing of the others, was different. The *Savannah* had scarcely been able to carry enough coal for one-eighth of its journey-time.

Could anyone hope to do better? Several optimists attempted it, with

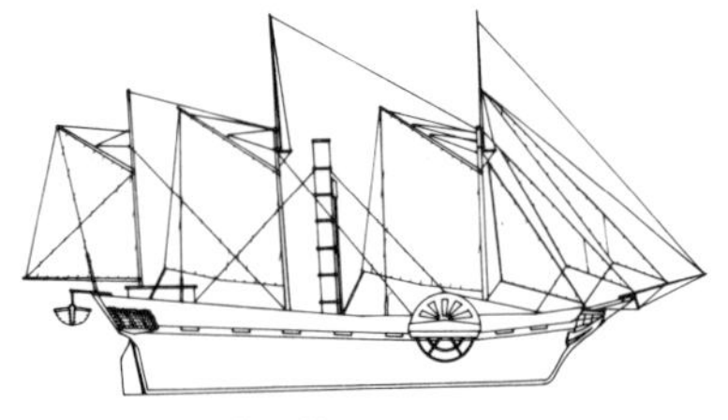

The *Curacao*.

varying degrees of success. In 1827, the *Curacao*, first steamship in the Netherlands Navy, lurched, and splashed, and sailed over a route from Holland to the West Indies, losing paddle-floats with monotonous regularity. Her opposite number in the British Navy, the *Rhadamanthus*, made a similar trip from England to Barbados in 1833. In the same year, seven stalwart passengers paid £20 each to cross from Quebec to Britain on board the paddle-steamer *Royal William*. The *William* steamed all the way — but this was not quite the breakthrough it appeared. Every four days, she would stop for twenty-four hours while the salt was cleaned from her boilers. In all, the crossing took nearly a month, and the fee-payers aboard might just as well have gone by sail. A similarly qualified success greeted attempts to steam to India, either via the Cape or on the Bombay-Aden leg of the Overland Route. Even when carrying coal in every possible nook and cranny, paddlers such as the *Hugh Lindsay* (alias the '*Waterlily*' — with fuel packed into her bunkers, her saloon and her passenger cabins, she sat so low in the water as to be almost awash) made terribly slow time. A steamer of 1836 called the *Berenice* managed a round-the-Cape voyage in three months, as opposed to the minimum of four a sailing-ship needed, but she wasted a sixth of that time in bunkering ports on the way.

In short, steam at that period was a dodgy venture. The commercial rewards for success were great, but the chances of failure were even greater. The most anyone aspired to was a steam-and-sail auxiliary arrangement, with the question of which was auxiliary to which being left to the demands of circumstance. The reality of non-stop ocean passage powered entirely by steam seemed distant indeed.

All the same, a breakthrough was soon to come, and it would come on the Atlantic. It was primarily the work of three outstanding men, backed by support such as only they proved able to command.

There were an Englishman, an American and a Canadian. Isambard Kingdom Brunel was an engineer of genius; Junius Smith, a barrister, businessman and frequent transatlantic traveller who had the vision to conceive of transatlantic steam travel as a practical possibility; and Samuel Cunard, a prodigy who, while still under age, set up the shipping firm of Abraham Cunard and Son (Abraham was his father) and never looked back afterwards. Each of the three was associated with a ponderously-named steamship firm: Brunel and the Great Western Steamship Company, Smith and the British and American Steam Navigation Company, Cunard and the British and North American Royal Mail Steam-Packet Company — later, and inevitably, to be known simply by the name of its main promoter. The first two concerns went bust over a hundred years ago; Cunard owns the *Queen Elizabeth II*. And yet, compared with the other two, Cunard's company was a Johnny-come-lately. Samuel Cunard was a canny and cautious man; when, ten years after the *Savannah*'s crossing, he was invited to

Opposite: Samuel Cunard.

S Cunard

The *Great Western*.

interest himself in steam, he allowed that 'We are entirely unacquainted with the cost of a steam boat, and would not like to embark in a business of which we are quite ignorant.' He later remedied the gaps in his knowledge very thoroughly — but, while he was at it, the other two stole a march on him.

The late 1830s saw the shipping worlds of London and New York in a state of something like frenzy. Times had changed since the *Savannah* had bucketed its way into public interest and out again; steam had become big news, and for a classic reason. The thing had suddenly turned sporting. Two ships — one built by British know-how, the other American-inspired — were to race across the Atlantic from Britain to New York, steaming all the way. The British nominee, Brunel's paddle-steamer *Great Western*, was nearly ready; the other, Junius Smith's *Royal Victoria* . . . . Well, what had happened to the *Victoria*? Her engines were still sitting, half-finished, in a Glasgow workshop; the engineering firm had gone bankrupt. Hastily, Smith looked round for something else, and found it: a small coastal steamer, considerably smaller than the *Great Western*, called the *Sirius*. The *Sirius*'s normal ports of call were London, Plymouth and Queenstown; to have her take in New York as well was a sporting venture in itself — but one that, against all the odds, paid off.

By the end of March 1838 both vessels were ready and waiting for their passengers. The *Great Western*, establishing a tradition in ship's decor that is still going strong, went in for wall decoration at its most grandiose: fifty large panels in the style of *ancien régime* France featuring country scenes, the arts and sciences, and 'parties grouped, or engaged in elegant sports and amusements'. There was also an artful system of bells, just as much a triumph of Victorian engineering as the ship that boasted it. The passenger, instead of bawling for a steward, merely pulled a bell-rope; in the steward's room, a bell rang in a box, and a small tin plate popped up showing the number of the room where assistance was needed. 'Thus,' noted the *Civil Engineer and Architect's Journal* of the day, 'instead of an interminable number of bells there are only two. This arrangement, which is alike ingenious as it is useful, is deserving the notice of architects.'

The *Sirius*, hurriedly dressed up for its role as trail-blazer, also had some elegant appointments: vast mirrors round the walls in the saloon and cabin refinements that, in the words of one visitor, would suit 'the most luxurious voluptuary'. And it was the attractions of the *Sirius* that drew the wider appreciation of the paying public. When, on 4 April, she finally set off across the Atlantic from Queenstown, she carried forty passengers, divided in the traditional manner between cabin class and steerage. The *Great Western*, departing from Bristol four days later, carried only seven.

The *Great Western* would, in fact, have carried more if it had not been for an accident that took place as she left London River for the first leg of her journey west. The lagging round her boilers caught fire. The flare-up that followed came near to costing the Great Western Company not only its first steam vessel but also the life of its most notable associate. Brunel, who had started the whole venture by jokingly suggesting that the Great Western Railway should have a ship to meet the train at Bristol, tried to climb down a half-burnt ladder, put his foot through a rung and fell eighteen feet into the boiler-room below. The fire was put out, Brunel was ferried to a doctor on shore, and the *Great Western* marked time in the Thames estuary until the tide could float her off. The *Sirius*, which had left London on 28 March, now had an even bigger lead and a name still untarnished. Round one to *Sirius*.

As far as landsmen were concerned, a gap then ensued. The ships bore up reasonably well; passengers coped with seasickness as best they could. 'The dreadful cry of "Steward — Steward" — the last ejaculation of despair — comes from a dozen nooks,' reported an observer; perhaps the 'ingenious' bell mechanism had got jammed through over-use.

Isambard Kingdom. Brunell, engineer of genius, photographed in front of the check chains of the *Great Eastern*.

On the night of 22 April, the people of New York went to bed as usual. They woke up to the news that the winner of the Great Race had arrived late the evening before, had spent the night on a mud-flat (there had been no pilot around to guide her in) and was even now paddling into harbour on the high tide. It was the *Sirius*. The little black and green coastal steamer, 208 feet long and weighing only 703

Winner . . . or runner-up? The *Sirius* arrives at New York.

tons against the *Great Western*'s 1320, had taken to the western ocean like the bird she most closely imitated. Indeed, 'behaving nobly and riding like a duck' was one verdict on her behaviour during one of the worst bits of the passage. The noble paddler had made the crossing in eighteen and a half days, and the best outward-bound average recorded for the sailing ships of the period was thirty and a half. She had, it seemed, exhausted her fuel and fallen back on chopped-up cabin furniture to last the course. (*Great Western* supporters nastily embroidered this tale by describing how the furnaces had been fed with, *inter alia*, toys torn from their sobbing owners.) But, all the same, she had won.

And then, when half New York had rushed down to the waterfront to cheer the new arrival, there was a diversion. Scarcely puffed, and with fuel to spare in plenty, the *Great Western*, too, was steaming up-harbour to her anchorage. The *Sirius* had arrived first, but her rival had arrived faster; the *Great Western* had made the crossing in fifteen and a quarter days flat.

Opposite: end of a pioneer. The *Sirius is* finally wrecked.

So Brunel and the Great Western Company had won after all. The fact got somewhat lost momentarily, however, among the parties,

THE "SIRIUS" STEAMER

THE "SIRIUS," AS LEFT BY THE TIDE.

CLEARING THE WRECK.

speeches, presentations and general hullabaloo that greeted the arrival of what a newspaperman on the other side of the Atlantic dubbed 'the great animals of the day'. No one reported geese flying over the grave when one worthy made the prophetic remark that 'steamers will continue to be the fashion until some more dashing adventurer of the go-ahead tribe shall demonstrate the practicability of balloon navigation, and gratify their impatience on a voyage *over*, and not *upon*, the blue waters in two days instead of as many weeks.' (It was not, in the event, a balloon that starred in the first air crossing but a Vickers Vimy bomber with fabric wings and Rolls-Royce engines, some eighty years later.)

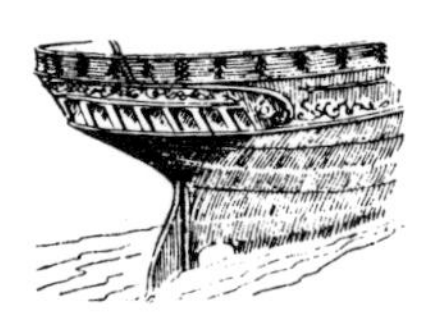

Early steamer sterns.
From top to bottom:
Teviot (1841); *Solent* (1853); *Shannon* (1874); *Deseado* (1911).

But prestige told almost immediately, and prestige was made by speed. For the return run, the *Great Western* netted a more respectable total of seventy-one passengers — and, just as important, 20,000 letters. The *Sirius* scooped only forty-nine people and 5500 items of mail. The Dog Star's namesake did, however, acquire an unlooked-for consolation prize in the shape of a testimonial from two passengers under sail whose ship encountered the *Sirius* out at sea. In the middle of dinner, three tedious weeks from land, the saloon's occupants were electrified to hear that a steamer was in sight astern. They dropped their napkins, gulped down their mouthfuls of roast fowl and rushed on deck. 'There she was sure enough — but a speck on the horizon — but with the line of black smoke above, leaving no doubt as to her character,' wrote eye-witness Judge Joseph Howe of Nova Scotia. 'On she came in gallant style with the speed of a hunter, while we were moving with the rapidity of an ox-cart loaded with marsh mud.' The *Sirius* agreed to take the England-bound mails that the brig was carrying, and Howe and his companion, Judge Thomas Haliburton, cadged a ride on the mailbags as they were rowed across by tender from one ship to the other. 'While these were handed up the side,' Howe noted, 'we had five minutes to chat with the passengers on the quarterdeck of the *Sirius*, and to take a glass of Champagne with her Commander in the cabin. She had been fourteen days making a much longer passage than we had made in twenty — she would reach England in two and a half or three days certain, we might be a week or a fortnight, or, with a spell of easterly weather, three weeks more.' It required, he added, a 'strong effort' to tear themselves away and return to the slow and spartan *Tyrian*, 'not at all pleased with the prospects of being left behind to the tender mercies of wind and canvas, when a few tons of coal would have done the business much better'.

It was a thoughtful pair of justices that watched the *Sirius* paddle off towards the horizon. (True to form, she all but ran out of coal again, and her landfall was dramatic. Fogbound, she nearly wrecked herself on one of the Scilly Isles.) Howe had summed the whole thing up in his comparison of the journey-times the *Tyrian* and the *Sirius* were

The paddle-steamer *Trent* piles on sail.

respectively making. The advantages steam could bring to trade, to passenger travel and to the key Nova Scotia port of Halifax were obvious – and it already seemed as though the Canadians might be left out. On arrival in England, these fears looked to be confirmed; it emerged that the British government was considering the possibility of awarding the country's transatlantic mail services, backed by a subsidy, to a steamship line, plying between Britain and *either* Halifax or New York. And rumour had it that New York was the more probable choice. Feeling, nevertheless, that steamships in any port were a better option than sail, the two Nova Scotia judges dashed off a petition to Whitehall. Howe also met and lunched with a prominent fellow-countryman, Sam Cunard.

In November 1838, six months after the Great Race had proved what steam could do, the Nova Scotians' fears were dispelled. The government invited tenders for a steamship mail service that would call at both New York and Halifax. (The year before, a similar contract for mails going to Gibraltar had been awarded to P & O's forerunner, the Peninsular Steam Navigation Company.) The transatlantic service, the invitation for tender announced, was to be carried out by steamers of not less than 300 horsepower, and it was to begin on 1 April 1839.

It was obvious that the Great Western Company would tender. The *Great Western* itself was now making regular trips across the Atlantic. A second *Royal William*, chartered by a Liverpool firm, had undertaken a few trips, rather in the *Sirius* style — one landing at New York had been achieved thanks to using wood from the spars and decks as fuel, the coal having run out. The same firm had also launched the brand-new *Liverpool* (which was, however, to prove an unlucky ship).

Dockside farewells; in the background, a Black Ball Line poster.

And Junius Smith's ship, once called the *Royal Victoria* but now renamed the *British Queen*, was all but completed. One of them looked sure to get the mail-carrying job and the crucially important cash grant. Then, quite suddenly, a figure previously all but unknown came on the scene. Hitherto, Cunard's chief claim to fame in Britain was that he was the Halifax representative of the East India Company. He had also set up a mail service between Halifax, Boston and Bermuda. By the year of the Great Race, he was thoroughly acquainted with the possibilities of steam. 'Steamers properly built and manned,' he commented in 1838, contradicting his earlier views on the subject, 'might start and arrive at their destination with the punctuality of railroad trains on land.' Early in 1839, he arrived in Britain (by sailing packet) with one aim in mind: to win the mail contract for himself. Through drive, contacts and business acumen he succeeded. Both *Sirius* and the *Great Western* had made gallant efforts, but the real winner of the Great Race was a concern that had been present at neither the start nor the finishing-post.

The award of the mail contract was, however, the signal for a far bigger and much more desperate race to start. At a time when steamers regularly using the western ocean could be counted on the fingers of two hands, the numbers of their sailing packet competitors ran into hundreds if not thousands. Though at the mercy of the weather as regards their arrival times, they too departed with punctuality from their appointed berths; in fact, they had invented the whole idea. And, at their best, they could achieve fantastic speeds. The *Canada* had made its phenomenal west-east run in fifteen days, eighteen

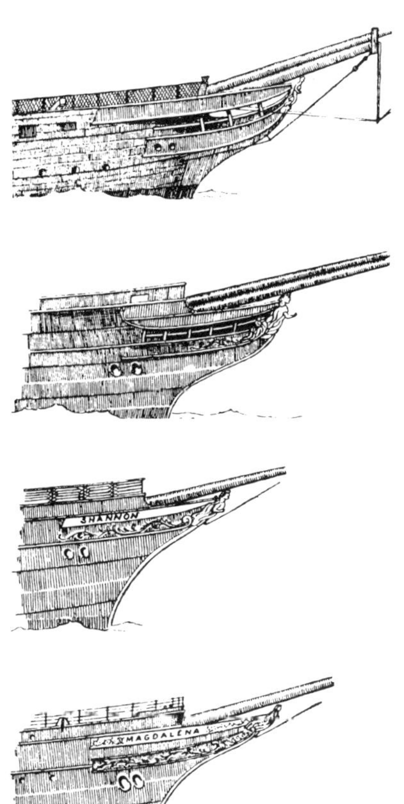

Early steamer bows. From top to bottom: *Trent* (1841); *Tasmanian* (1859); *Shannon* (1871); *Magdalena* (1889).

hours; a race in the same direction between the *Columbus* and the *Sheridan* (with $10,000 staked on the outcome) was won by the *Columbus* with a crossing only a few hours longer. The *Independence*, built a full year before Brunel made his light-hearted suggestion to the Great Western Railway's directors, more than once did the New York-Liverpool trip in fourteen days only. The record for the much more arduous east-west voyage was seized by a packet called the *Yorkshire*, whose sixteen-day run compares favourably with that of the *Sirius* itself. Until steam came, the packets were the undisputed lords of the North Atlantic.

Their supremacy had begun in 1816, as trade and potential passenger interest picked up after the ravages of the Napoleonic Wars. And the initiative went to the Americans. Before then, hardy souls wishing to cross the Atlantic and other oceans foraged around for a ship that was going in their direction and then waited until it had enough freight and passengers (especially freight) to make sailing worthwhile. In contrast, the newly-formed Black Ball Line service offered a regular fast crossing between New York and Liverpool, leaving on the first and sixteenth of each month come what might. Despite the high price of the trip — thirty-five guineas per cabin passenger — the venture was a roaring success, and other packet lines speedily sprang up. (As the soubriquet 'packet' indicated, the Black Ballers were also entrusted with delivery of the mails.) Soon, the Black Ball flag (crimson swallowtail with a black ball centred) was in cut-throat rivalry with that of the Swallowtail Line (red/white or blue/white swallowtails), the Dramatic Line (blue above white, with twin Ls) and the Black X (red swallowtail with Black X centred). The *Canada* and *Yorkshire* were Black Ballers, the *Independence* a Swallowtail. The extraordinary turns of speed put up by these three were the direct result of the lines' rivalry. The mails by themselves were a profitable enough cargo, but people were soon to prove an even better one. As the nineteenth century progressed into its third decade, the totals of emigrants hoping to leave poverty and starvation behind them in the Old World reached an annual 50,000 — and went on climbing. However little each individual steerage passenger paid for the trip — between four and eight guineas — the emigrants collectively presented a glittering prize, one which the Black Ballers and the rest would not give up without a struggle.

They might not offer the all-weather speed and reliability of the steamers (proofs of which, in the early days, were in any case rather inconclusive). They certainly could not boast refinements such as stewards, bells and paintings after Watteau. But the emigrant trade was too valuable to lose, and the sailing packet lines' fight to keep it led them to adopt sometimes drastic methods.

3. *'They Sing Like Birds'*

Among the deluge of advice that was showered upon prospective emigrants to America during the last century was a slim volume produced in 1830 by the British radical William Cobbett. He was no armchair commentator; he had made the Atlantic crossing himself, and had returned. 'It grieves me very much to know it to be my duty to publish this book,' he wrote in his publicity puff, 'but I cannot refrain from doing it, when I see the alarms, and hear the cries of thousands of virtuous families that it may save from utter ruin.'

One way of avoiding 'ruin' — his choice of words, as events showed, was no exaggeration — was to sail American. American packets, Cobbett said, were faster, better and safer than any others, and the reason lay in the superiority of their captains. He went on:

> I never knew an American captain take off his clothes to go to bed during the whole voyage; and I never knew any other who did not do it. The consequence of this great watchfulness is that, advantage is taken of every puff of wind, while the risk from the squalls and sudden gusts is, in a great measure, obviated . . . . A drinking, sleeping fellow would have done one of two things: keep out the sails during the squalls, and have his sails and rigging torn to pieces, and have been retarded on his voyage; or, he would have taken in his sails in the evening at any rate, and just kept on at two or three miles an hour, instead of eight or ten miles an hour, during the night.

Cobbett may have allowed his pen to run away with him on the subject of the captains' sleeping habits, but he had certainly got the general message, which was 'Speed and nothing spared'. Speed was the key: to publicity, to longer passenger lists, to percentages on fatter and still fatter pay-offs. The packet captains, most of whom had a financial share in their ships, were professionals through and through — but, not unreasonably, they also believed in full payment for their services. Their special dues were 25 per cent on cabin fares, 5 per cent on steerage payments, 5 per cent on freight charges, and the twopence-a-letter mail allowance (the American rate was two cents). As far as their upper-class passengers went, they presented an image that combined the best features of Nelson and Henry VIII: bluff masters of the drawing-room, of the table and of the poop-deck. Underneath the *bonhomie*, however, they were iron-minded despots who refused to spare either themselves or others.

To meet his punishing schedules, the 'Old Man' of a sailing packet relied on three things: his skill, the strength of his ship and the strong arms of his first, second and third mates. These, on the western ocean, had significant names; the second mate was called the 'blower' ('blow', as in *Blow the Man Down*, meant knock, fell or smash) and number three was the 'striker'. Particularly grim individuals were known by more specific titles: Kicking Jack Williams, Saccarappa ('The Undertaker') Joe and Boss-eyed Bill the Bowery Bastard. Their job was to direct, co-ordinate and control the crew — above all, control it.

Cobbett, despite his radical views, took a quite ludicrously rosy view of the common sailor's lot. It was his theory that sailors actually *liked* bad weather on the grounds that it meant less work for them. They were, he said, 'never so happy as when tied by ropes to the bulwarks for fear of being washed overboard, and when all the sails and yards are taken down and stowed away, and when the masts are lowered to the lowest possible point. Tied to the bulwarks, they sing like birds in a shrubbery.' They sang, certainly, but to say that they were happy, in fair weather or foul, was complete nonsense. A crack packet was run on much the same lines as a crack regiment of the period; the idea was to inspire so much fear in the men that they forgot to be frightened of the enemy. The wretched 'packet rats' were the sweepings of seaport slums all round the world — multilingual, illiterate, violent, brutish — and they were treated brutishly. Their quarters were dark, leaking triangular spaces in the bows of the ship, sometimes provided with bunks, sometimes not. Their food was ship's biscuit and hunks of salt meat. Their work was unbelievably hard and dangerous, and the punishments that met any kind of failure were also, to our present-day minds, unbelievable. They were worked over with knuckledusters, fists, buckets and iron belaying-pins (with a sour attempt at humour they called this particular treatment 'belaying-pin soup'). They were tarred and feathered. They were forced to pull iron nails out of the deck with their teeth. To the paying public, the Black Ballers and the rest were fine vessels, commanded by fearless and gallant men. To Packet-rat Johnny (all merchant seamen were dubbed John; it was the Navy that spawned Jolly Jack), they were hellships or bloodboats, to be boarded only at great need and to be left as soon as possible.

Jumping ship after a one-way voyage was common, but, desperate remedy though it was, it too often gave a respite even more temporary than intended. For a consideration, the owners of seamen's boarding-houses undertook to act as one-man press-gangs; they drugged their lodgers' drinks or embroiled them in debt, and the result, either way, was the same. Within hours, the shanghaied sailor would be back at

Hoisting sail in the Atlantic.

sea, fuddled, retching and penniless, his last port a mere blur on the horizon. Protests brought instant retribution, even death; the mates' power was such that they could, and did, get away with murder. There were few, on land or sea, minded to speak up for the ordinary sailor, and those who tried were usually ignored. This was a hell there was no escaping from.

Yet, in an indirect way, the packet rats managed to speak up for themselves. Furthermore, they managed it under the very noses of the authorities they so feared. By an ironic twist of circumstances, they had been granted a licence to criticise by the very same economic pressures that were all but killing them.

What had given the seamen their weapon was the rediscovery, early on in the sailing packet period, of a fact that had been almost forgotten after centuries of naval veto: that groups of men worked better if they were allowed to sing at the same time. As a time-and-motion technique, it was reckoned to be worth six extra hands on a rope, and captain and mates all recognised good business when they saw it. So, as Cobbett noted, the men sang — and filled their songs with formalised protest that would, if merely spoken aloud, have brought catastrophe. The

Cutty Sark, one of the great cargo-clippers.

English language shanty (or chanty, or chantey) came into being — an aid to greater efficiency, a method of striking back at Striker, a highly-coloured and devastating record of life as the packet rat saw it, a symbolic catalogue of his hopes and fears.

In the century or more since their birth, shanties have sustained some rough handling. Except among the experts, they are now things of embarrassment; memories of *The Mermaid*, *A-Roving*, and *The Golden Vanitee* will today make ninety-nine people out of a hundred remember some school concert — and cringe. The credentials as true shanties of both *Vanitee* and *Mermaid* are dubious, however, and this may explain the way they relentlessly appear at organised children's sing-ups. For the truth is that the shanty proper is totally unsuited to drawing-room or camp-fire treatment. The ones that we all know have been tidied up, in both words and tune, almost beyond recognition; the authentic version of *A-Roving*, for example, has a marked similarity to *Roll Me Over in the Clover*, while some verses of the shanty *The Hog-Eye Man* are so extraordinary that they are locked away in a sex research institute in Indiana. Unless shanties were sung within the hearing of first-class passengers (and the mates usually drew the line at that) there was absolutely no call for them to be polite. On the contrary, they were intended first to catch the interest and second to provide a rhythm to which tedious manual tasks could be effectively performed.

Nearly always, the shanty proper was a song for soloist and chorus

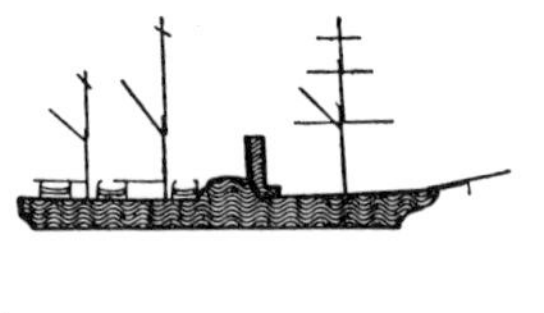

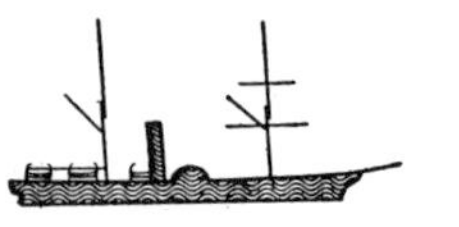

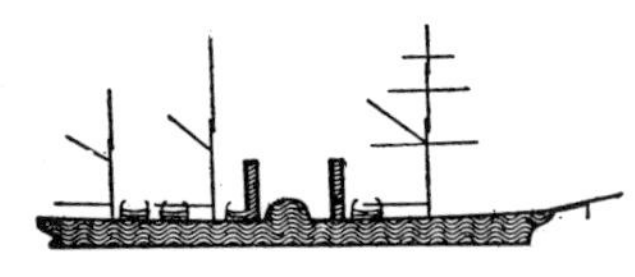

Early steamers . . . (*Forth*, 1841; *Conway*, 1846; *Solent*, 1853).

rather than for a group, and this soloist was expected to be something of a virtuoso. In the early days, at least, he seldom put a hand to a rope himself. His only job was to get the men moving and keep them that way, by picking the right shanty for the task in hand, by extending it through improvisation and borrowings from other songs to last the task through, and by timing his delivery to match the nature of the effort involved. His material knew no geographical boundaries; a shanty evolved on the western ocean packets would drift southwards to the Caribbean, and work-songs from the South Atlantic would find their way north. A top-class performer would throw in trills, vocal jumps and twiddly-bits for extra effect; negroes and Scandinavians were particularly good at this. A modern recording of *Day-O* — itself a worksong — gives a faint idea of classic shanty style.

At its most basic, a shanty went something like this:

Oh, Juli*a*!
Pretty Miss Juli*a*!
Take 'em off, Juli*a*!
Lay back Juli*a*!

The shantyman would improvise as many remarks on Julia as the occasion warranted; at the syllables in italics, the hands would join in with a grunt and a massive heave. The sequence was used when a few good hauls were needed to get a rope taut.

More complicated, but still on the terse side, was *Sally Rackett* (again, the chorus was shouted rather than sung):

Little Sally Rackett,
Haul 'er away!
She shipped in a packet,
Haul 'er away!
An' she never did regret it,
Haul 'er away!
Wid a *Hauly* high-*ho*!

A third laconic work-song was used exclusively when the flopping ton-weight of topsail had to be gathered on to its yard for furling. Balanced high above the decks and clutching armfuls of soaking canvas, the seamen on the job would gasp out:

Ter me way-ay-hay-high-*yah*!
We'll pay Paddy Doyle for his *boots*!

Paddy Doyle was a boarding-house keeper who — doubtless by accident — once let something go for nothing. Other verses dealt with drink, the captain and the cook. As in *Julia*, the grunt and heave came at the end of the line; more than three verses were seldom needed.

Most jobs, however, called for a lot more than that. Manpower was sure, but it was also slow. Ten verses was about average for a shanty, although epics of twenty or more were not uncommon. One of these celebrated the mythical Stormalong, or Old Stormy, the archetypal 'good skipper' and the seamen's equivalent of King Arthur. His birthplace was in the sailing-ships' hell of Cape Horn; his funeral was in heroic style:

Lower him down with a golden chain,
Carry him *along*, boys, carry him *along*.
Make sure he don't rise again,
Carry him *to* the burying *ground*.

The shanty — a slow, measured one — was used for the endless trudge round the capstan.

Another folk-hero (and one who, in a tidied-up version, has found his way into the song-books) was Reuben Ranzo, the stubbornest, lubberliest, grimiest sailor in the world. Ranzo's fortunes were complicated and varied according to the singers, but one element remained constant. He was tied to a grating and:

They have him lashes thirty
*Ran*zo, boys, *Ran*zo!
Because he was so dirty,
*Ran*zo, boys — *Ran*zo!

However, he married the captain's daughter and ended up with his own ship.

Stormy and Reuben were unusual in that they were proper heroes in every sense of the word. As was inevitable, given the circumstances under which he lived, the seaman's attitude to his symbolised world was normally one of extreme scepticism. Most women in the shanties are whores, shipmates fools or bastards, foreigners simply peculiar, the mates, to a man, drunken swine. But it was, on the whole, wisest to avoid direct comment on real-life, here-and-now personnel within their hearing. One western ocean shantyman had improvised on the favourite *Bowline* ('Haul on the bowline, Sally is me darlin'') shanty by inserting the line 'Captain he's a-growlin''; the two mates set upon him and knocked him unconscious.

On the other hand, one shanty was recognised as conveying a permissible hint that things could be improved. *Whisky Johnny* was usually sung at the top-gallant or topsail halyards. The actual verses frequently strayed from the main theme, and a lot appeared to preach temperance. One set went:

Now if ye ever go to 'Frisco town,
Mind you steer clear of Shanghai Brown.
He'll dope yer whisky night and morn
And then shanghai ye round Cape Horn.

But the message conveyed in each line of the chorus — 'Whisky for my Johnny!' — was unmistakable. A tot of rum would be appreciated.

Another shanty which took hope rather than fear as its theme was *The Dead Horse*. It was devised for a special ceremony which was staged at the end of the first month at sea. The point was that crew members, when they were signed on for a voyage, were given a one-month 'advance' note on their wages, intended to help them buy

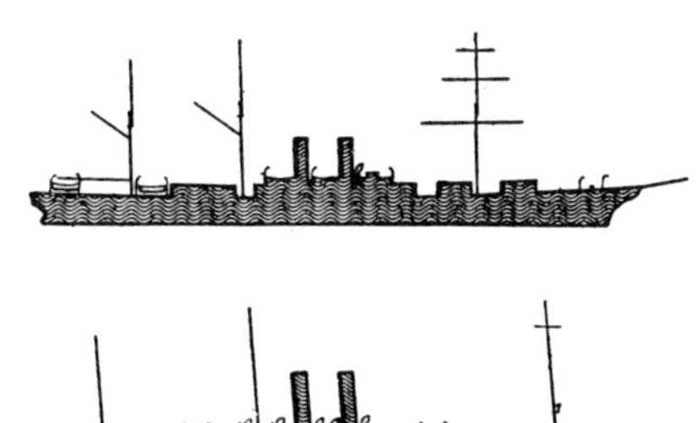

. . . and later ones (*Medway*, 1877; *Danube*, 1893).

their gear for the trip. But this was usually spent in pubs and brothels, and so the first month's work on board was 'work for a dead horse' — for nothing.

At the end of the month, though, work became worthwhile again. The dead horse could be paid off, and it was around this payment that the ceremony was built. Beforehand, the sail-maker would construct a dummy horse out of canvas, stuff it with old bits of rope, and weigh it with some of the sandstone blocks that were used for scrubbing down decks. On the day itself, the horse would be lugged along the deck and attached to a line from the main yard-arm. Hand over hand, it would be hauled aloft to where, with legs twisted round the yard and a knife in his hand, the youngest crew member was perched waiting. The climax came when a seaman on deck fired off a blue flare; the lad with the knife reached down, cut the rope and dropped the horse into the sea. The shanty was used for the hauling stage:

> We'll sink him down with a long, long roll,
> An' we *say* so! An' we *hopes* so!
> Where the sharks'll have his body, an' the devil have his soul,
> Oh *poor* old *hoss*!

There are at least sixteen other verses. It was a long haul, and, besides, the occasion was important.

Again, as far as captain and mates were concerned, the ceremony was good business; in modern terms, it boosted crew productivity. The crew themselves knew all about other ways of doing this. Unsurprisingly, the record-breaking packets were a favourite target for attack, and the shantyman's licence to exaggerate does nothing to hide the bitterness of such lines as:

> 'Tis larboard an' starboard on deck ye will sprawl,
> For Kicking Jack Williams commands this Blackball.

It was the Black Ballers that made such a feature of 'handspike hash' and 'belaying-pin soup'. It was the Black Ballers, too, that collected a particularly rich mixture of shanghaied amateurs:

> There's tinkers an' tailors an' sodgers an' all
> All ship as prime seamen aboard the Blackball.

Kicking Jack, whatever Cobbett may have thought, sent the terrified men aloft with the toe of his boot, and that was only a start. Once the ship was well at sea, the pace hotted up:

> 'An now when she's clear over old Mersey bar,
> The mate knocks 'em down with a big capstan-bar.

Nearly all variants of the Blackball Line shanty somewhere contain the comment:

> That's the Line where ye can shine,
> That's the Line where I wasted my prime . . .

and several continue, more subtly, with:

> They'll carry ye along through the ice an' snow,
> They'll take ye where the winds don't blow.

Opposite: cabin passengers watch as the 'dead horse' is prepared for burial.

'Where the winds don't blow' was a shantyman's euphemism for death. Old Stormy was there already.

But even the Blackball Line was better than the terrible Guinea Coast slave ship, American like the Black Ballers but plying its trade between the States and the Congo river. The shanty of the *Guinea Slaver*, or *Blow, Boys, Blow*, took John's worst fears and imaginings and wove them into a nightmare canvas. According to different singers, ship's rations here included 'mosquito hearts and sandflies' liver', 'water soup but slightly thinner', or 'monkey's tail and sweet potatoes'. The commanding hierarchy were devils from hell — Big Black Jack, Bully Forbes, Long John Hathaway from Arizona, and others. In the hold, the slaver's cargo of so-called 'black sheep' moaned and despaired; in the background came the boom of guns from the pursuing law-enforcement vessel.

How d'ye know she's a Yankee clipper?
Blow, boys, *blow*.
By the blood and guts that flow from her scuppers,
Blow, me bully boys, *blow*.

Today, only one shanty collection connects the Blackball Line with this vision of horror. But as far as techniques of command and discipline went, there was little to choose between one ship and another. On slaver and packet alike, the commanders had made the 'speed equals cash' equation, though with different aims in mind. The slaver intended to outstrip the law, the packet captain to satisfy his customers. Both earned their living by ruthlessly exploiting the laws of supply and demand, and those same laws ensured that they would never lack for a labour force. In one of the many *Hilo* shanties (Hilo is a port in Peru), the merchant seaman composed his own epitaph:

He signed for two pound ten a month,
Away! Hi*lo*!
No more than two pound ten a month,
Tom's gone to Hi*lo*!

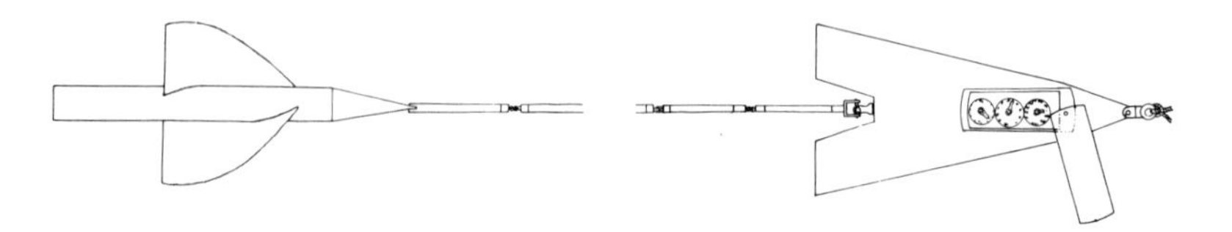

The ship's 'speedometer' — Massey's Log developed in the early nineteenth century.

4. *Under Sail*

Imagine seven London buses lined up end to end. Then visualise another bus and a half arranged crosswise at the centre of the row. Those were the dimensions of a larger-than-average sailing-packet of the nineteenth century. And within that space up to one thousand people would try to exist for five, six or seven weeks as their ship hammered its way across the Atlantic to New York or Canada. If they went on the record-beating *Yorkshire* — which offered, as extra inducement, the 'kindness and attention' shown to passengers by her commander, Captain Bailey — their time of trial would be shorter; the *Yorkshire*'s average for the 'uphill' east-to-west run was four weeks and one day.

The smallness of ships in pre-steam days is so obvious a fact that it tends to be passed over almost without comment. By present-day standards, they were tiny. A modern channel steamer measures about 385 feet from stern to bows and 65 feet across the beam; the *Yorkshire*'s vital statistics were 166½ feet by 36 feet. The iron sailing-ships that, well after steam had arrived on the North Atlantic run, were taking British emigrants out to Australia and New Zealand were in the region of 300 feet (or ten London buses) long. Passengers could well find that this became their home for three months or more.

Unbelievable though it seems today, small ships were not necessarily dangerous ships. Centuries of practical experience meant that sailing-ship design could be judged to a nicety, according to the sort of weather that the ship could be expected to meet. Clippers were built to take advantage of every gust of the Trade Winds they depended on; their bows tapered sharply, their spars towered. The packets, by contrast, were squatter, sturdier and — despite the pressure for speed — slower. To take on the North Atlantic in clipper style, with clouds of canvas aloft and foaming seas across the bows, was asking for trouble.

None the less, despite all the skill of the designer, shipwrecks were frequent: so frequent that they would daze us if they occurred on that scale today. Ships ran into icebergs, were smashed under by heavy seas

The emigrant ship *Ocean Monarch* burns in the Mersey estuary.

(the highest wave recorded in the Atlantic was eighty-nine feet high), caught fire, ran aground. Some of the most harrowing accounts of shipwrecks are those which tell how hundreds drowned within touching distance of land. The *Powhattan* went down with no survivors within eight yards of the low-water mark on the New Jersey coast. Would-be rescuers on shore held shouted conversations with the doomed passengers before she went down. The *Ocean Monarch*, one of the stars of the White Diamond Line, caught fire in the Mersey estuary and sank, taking 176 people with her. Just how close she was to land is shown by the fact that a sailor from a ship berthed in Liverpool managed to swim out to the burning wreck and help the last handful of survivors into rescue boats. Three-quarters of the *Annie Jane*'s 351 passengers died when she ran into a skerry in the Hebrides; 'The deck above our heads was bending like a sheet of paper', wrote a survivor, 'and threatening to fall and crush us every instant.' One sailing-ship in every six came to grief — but, of course, this did not mean that one voyage in every six ended in disaster. Whatever happened to the ships in the end — and their working lives were likely to be short — individual vessels lasted long enough for tens of thousands of passengers to complete the ocean passage each year. And one ship at least proved that her builders had got their designs supremely right; she lasted for twenty-nine years, made 116 round trips between Britain and America and never lost a single hand. (In fact, as far as passengers went, she even gained; during her three decades in the business, 1500 babies were born on board.)

Barring accidents, then (and, as the *Titanic* and others were later to prove, accidents happen to sail and steamships alike, however well-appointed the latter were), the tough little packet boats and the glamorous clippers offered a relatively safe method of making the 3000-mile trip from Liverpool to New York or the very much longer one via the Cape of Good Hope from London to Sydney. What they did *not* offer was comfort — comfort, that is, as passengers on the *QE2*, or a Channel steamer, or even a hovercraft would understand it. Sea-travellers under sail lived out their voyages under conditions of either cramped tedium or horrifying squalor; which they opted for depended on the length of their purses.

On board a nineteenth-century ship, as on land, people were strictly divided into two nations. You were cabin trade, or you were steerage. The cabins were usually in the stern or in a special deck-house; steerage quarters consisted of long rows of berths in the space immediately under the main open-air deck. Access to these was via narrow hatchways. In theory, preparations for your passage to America, Bombay or Auckland began well in advance. 'If your wife has been accustomed to have servants,' Cobbett says, 'it will be absolutely necessary to dismiss them' — adding the suggestion that a servantless three months or so is good training for self-sufficiency. But in practice only the cabin trade could afford a shopping list that, in the longest runs of all, through the Indian Ocean, included furniture.

Moving into your cabin — if it was twelve feet square you had got exceptionally good value — was like moving house; indeed, it *was* moving house, by slow stages. The furniture you sat on, wrote on and slept on at sea would form the nucleus of a drawing-room or bedroom suite in your new home in a far-flung outpost of the Empire.

Emigrants board a ship bound for Australia.

Leave-takings, as seen by Victorian painter Abraham Solomon.

Bearing in mind that split cane was the nineteenth-century equivalent of plastic — hard-wearing, water-resistant, lightweight, with the added advantage that it did not stick to the skin in hot weather — the furnishings that eastbound cabin passengers took with them on their ninety-day haul were extremely practical: cane-backed chairs, beds with cane headboards, brass-bound sea-chests for storage. In Canterbury Museum, Christchurch, New Zealand, there is a reconstruction of a cabin shared by James and Fanny Fitzgerald, who in 1850 paid £84 for what was then a luxury cabin passage to New Zealand. For their money, they got the additional advantages of a large stern window and a private water closet. To get one of these made a long voyage infinitely more tolerable, especially for women. For them, the only alternative consonant with decorum was a chamber-pot. The Fitzgeralds took with them, among other things, a double-bed, a settee with basketwork back and sides, an easy chair, a writing-desk, various boxes and trunks, candle lamps and their bedding. All this, along with the Fitzgeralds themselves and Fanny's hooped skirts, was crammed into a space eleven feet by nine.

On the Atlantic packets, however, basic furniture was laid on for the price of the ticket. Carpets, chairs, twin bunks with curtains, wash-basins that fitted into a special stand with holes in the top, drawers whose special fastenings ensured that they would stay shut when the ship moved: all these were displayed for the dazzlement and ease of the well-to-do. The main saloon, on to which the cabins usually opened, had further attractions such as bulging plush sofas, stuffed with horsehair, and a wealth of stained, silvered and frosted glass. After the cabins, the saloon was pleasingly big: thirty-five feet by fifteen was very handsome, and a ceiling 'high enough for any man under eight feet in his boots' was thought most modern.

For cabin passengers on the Atlantic and Eastern runs alike, the saloon was the heart of the ship. It was here that they ate, drank, socialised, played cards, dominoes or chess, betted on the time the journey would take.

It was here, too, that they tried to control the first sweating, lurching pangs of seasickness. If this got too bad — and it was a lucky passenger who escaped it altogether — they were hauled off to their cabins, handed their chamber-pots, and left to throw up in comparative solitude. On average, they remained in this condition for ten days or

Shipboard scene, 1840s.

A party of 'distressed needlewomen' are prepared for the voyage. Note arrangements for eating and sleeping.

so; sixteen — a fortnight or more of misery — was reckoned to be the limit. Children turned out to be better sailors than their parents.

It was only in the wake of the Second World War that an end was put to the nightmare that the vast majority of sea-passengers, rich or poor, had to go through before reaching dry land again. An antihistamine drug called dimenhydrinate had been developed by an allergy clinic in Baltimore and given to a woman suffering primarily from hives and incidentally from tramcar-sickness. It cured both — and the US Army, more interested in the seasickness angle than in the allergy, decided to test the new product on troops being ferried to Germany across the North Atlantic. Not one of those given Dramamine, the proprietary name of the new drug, was ill, while soldiers in a control group, dosed on sugar placebos, lay around the corridors in wretched heaps.

There can be few air, sea, or car-travellers who have not since had cause to bless the researchers of Baltimore and the Army guinea-pigs. All the other palliatives have proved so hopeless. In the nineteenth century these included:

warm clothing
plenty to eat
nothing to eat
beef tea
mustard plasters
essence of peppermint
fresh lemons
rum
abstinence from strong drink

sea-water (taken both internally and externally)
prayer
a suspended cabin whose movements compensated for those of the ship (an unsuccessful invention of steel pioneer Henry Bessemer)
fat bacon
'physic' (seaport chemists must have made a fortune)
fresh air.

Some of these — notably fresh air and peppermint — are certainly better than nothing; others sound worse than useless. There must, however, have been *something* about fat smoked pig as a remedy for nausea; as late as the turn of the century, expectant mothers were being advised to take a little ham to counter their early-morning sickness. But fresh air, paradoxically, was one of the hardest things to come by on a ship on a rough passage. During bad weather, when passengers would not, in any case, have been likely to be welcomed on deck, shutters were put across such windows as they had and kept there as long as the storm lasted. The Fitzgeralds might well have lived by the light of gimbel-mounted candles for weeks on end.

Seasick cabin passengers who retained some element of analytical thought probably reflected sadly on another shipboard irony: the fact that, by virtue of their indisposition, they were unable to take part in

Between decks.

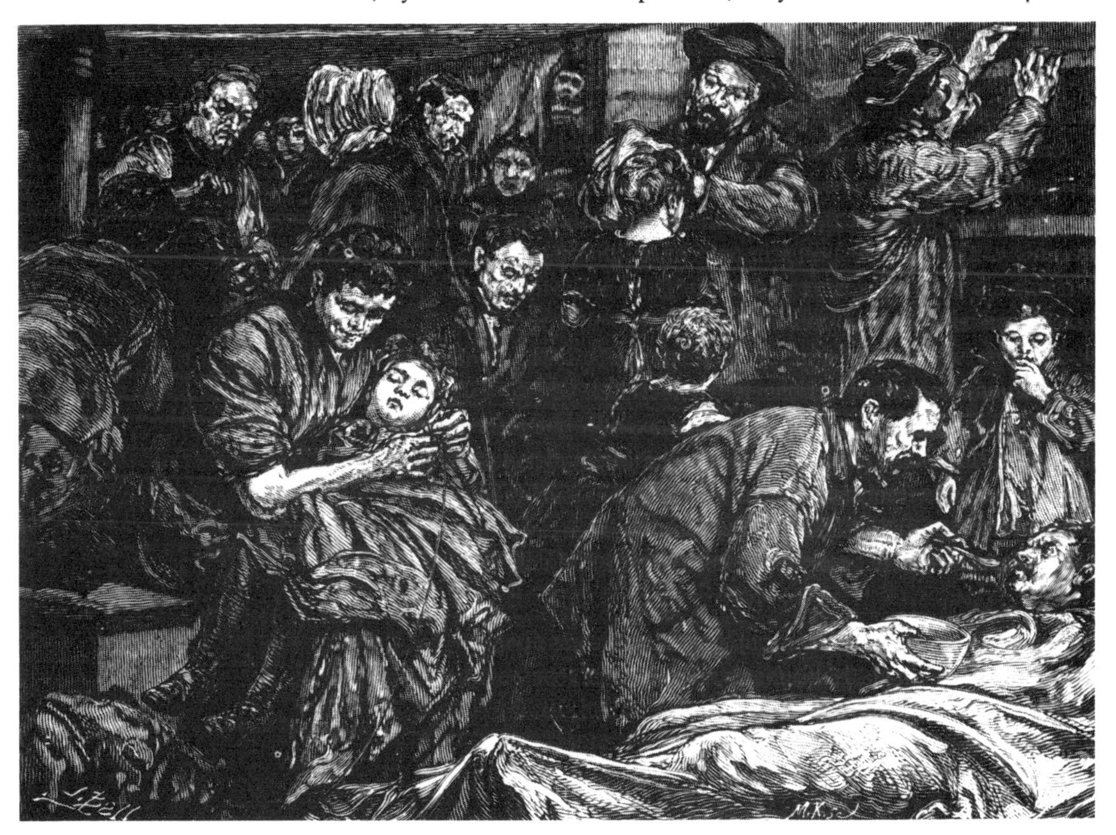

the one element of civilised life that ships did really well. The main tedium-reliever on a long journey was eating, and the food — if you could face it — was often excellent.

The main meal of the day was dinner, taken in the late afternoon and drawn out as long as possible. There was a certain jockeying for places at table, especially if the captain was dining; on the Indian Ocean ships, he would sit between the two senior ladies present. Travellers were advised not to eat so much at lunch that they could not do justice to the devilled fowl, legs of mutton, roast chicken, roast goose, roast pork or roast turkey that would be put before them later. Breakfast, unless one made a complete hog of oneself, was a lighter affair: ham, kippers, eggs, cutlets, bacon, tea, fresh rolls and a drop of strong liquor afterwards as a digestif.

And all of it — breakfast, lunch and dinner — was on the house. 'Far the best way', said Cobbett, adding that the only foodstuff that the cabin class should provide itself with in advance was a gallon of brandy. This monster ration was not aimed to act as a specific for *mal de mer* (Cobbett was one of those who prescribed abstinence, anyway) but to be 'judiciously administered in bribes to the black cook'.

Cobbett goes on: 'He would bid you toss your money into the sea, but he will suck down your brandy; and you will get many a nice thing prepared by him, which you would never get, if it were not for that brandy.'

Bribes for the cook apart, a good packet or colonial clipper carried all that its cabin passengers could reasonably want in the way of foodstuffs. The days of the floating hotel had not yet arrived, but the sailing ships did their best; in so far as space allowed, they were also floating farms. The problems of food preservation were overcome by shipping it live. There were cows for milk, chickens for eggs, sheep, pigs, geese, turkeys for meat. Some of them were housed in stalls and coops fixed up on the deck, others wandered about free. Whether they led happy lives or not is open to conjecture; Cobbett mentions 'seasick sheep, with eyes as white as those of whiting', but a passenger on a ship bound for New Zealand, later in the century, noted that the sheep 'are getting so tame they come and put their noses in our laps and rub about us like a pet dog'. Cobbett, however, had a rather jaundiced view about food and drink; the general opinion was that the meat nourished on fodder and salt-spray tasted not bad at all.

In addition, an ultimate luxury would sometimes be provided in the shape of fresh greenstuffs. When a ship's longboats were not offering accommodation to pigs, they might well be turned into glorified window-boxes. Sometimes, too, vegetables were planted on the ballast in the hold — a perfectly practical place for greenery that needed blanching. Manure, of course, was to be had in plenty. It was inevitable that, with all the food around, yet another form of nonpaying passenger should be present: every time a packet sailed quantities of rats sailed with her. Rat-hunts were an accepted way of passing the time.

With the exception of shipwreck, then, the most disagreeable experiences that could befall a cabin passenger during his month or more at sea were motion sickness, acute illness of other sorts (ships were supposed to carry surgeons but frequently did not), and a rat scurrying across the pillow. For those travelling steerage, however, things were much worse: indescribably so. Indeed, not even shipwreck could be counted as the final disaster, since death walked the jam-packed steerage quarters from the first day at sea.

A steerage passage to America on a packet ship cost between three and eight pounds, depending on the port of departure; London was more expensive than Liverpool. For that, the passenger got a place to sleep in (what sort of a place he did not discover until later) and his 'ship's allowance' of food: ship's biscuit, oatmeal, rice, flour, pork (perhaps), molasses, water. It was not wise, however, to count on the food side of the bargain. There was seldom enough; what there was had frequently gone off; and, in the scramble to grab some, to get water to cook it in, and then to secure a place at one of the very few cooking stoves provided, the weakest usually went to the wall.

Paddles have gone — but, as shown on this early poster, sail still remains.

A prudent steerage passenger who could afford to follow all the suggestions pressed on him would have presented himself at the dock encumbered with all the makings of a grocer's shop: flour, rice, salt, vinegar, apples, ham, potatoes, sugar, tea, eggs (packed in bran or salt), bread, coffee. In addition, he and his family would have been dressed in plenty of that Victorian cure-all, warm flannel, and somewhere near the surface of his baggage would have been a variety of tin basins, cups and plates — along with the indispensable chamber-pot.

All this, of course, presupposes that the steerage passenger could afford ham, flannel and coffee. Many could not. The majority of steerage passengers were all but penniless emigrants who, having somehow scraped together enough for their fares, had precious little left over for extras. Those who had food ate it as soon as their seasickness allowed them to; those who had nothing went without, petitioned their neighbours for charity, and — when and if they got their ship's allowance of meal — fought desperately for a place in the cook-stove queue.

The prudent passenger, if he knew what state his fellow-travellers were soon to find themselves in, would probably congratulate himself on his foresight and command of ready cash. But his complacency would not last for long. Two major problems — one immediate and the second long-term — were about to confront him. He had to get himself and his food-supply on board; and he had to keep both it and himself in good shape once they got there.

The *Taeping* ahead of the *Ariel* in the great tea clipper race of 1866.

Boarding could be a nightmare, especially when a ship refused to take passengers until the last minute, as many did since people got in the way of cargo-loading. People scrambled in hugger-mugger, pushing, pulling, being pushed in their turn; 'like so many bundles' commented one who had suffered. There was no question of an organised head-count at the top of the gangway; indeed, there could be no question of a definitive count of any sort until the ship was out of reach of land. Passengers would continue to scramble up the ship's sides even after it was in motion, and those who had missed their chance altogether could hire a boat — at a price — to take them out to the moving ship.

Once aboard, the steerage passenger would have been in no doubt as to where to go next. A constant stream of people like himself was disappearing through a narrow hatchway in the deck. Lugging his goods with him, he would have climbed down a steep ladder and wedged himself into his berth. For the next month or more he would sit, sleep, eat, vomit and, when there was no lavatory, or he was unable to use the one on the deck, void himself in a space six feet square and shared with three other people. Ventilation came from the hatchway, which in bad weather was clamped shut. Lights might well be forbidden on account of fire risks. If he had his family with him, they would naturally be his bedfellows; if he — or she — were single, he would be jammed in with total strangers of either sex. (This was later forbidden by law, but law and practice took some time to coincide.)

On each side of the newly-boarded passenger's berth would be others, stretching the length of the steerage compartment. Squashed into the six feet or so above them would be another row and possibly even a third. Open-fronted and open-sided, they were rickety affairs, usually knocked up out of any wood that was handy. The general effect was of row upon row of large hutches — hutches for humans. Even at the time, observers remarked on the similarities between the emigrant packets and the old-time slave ships.

If lavatories were provided (and they often were not) they were frequently on deck. During bad weather, steerage passengers were battened down in their quarters and managed as best they could. The smell of excrement and old vomit — never totally absent, even in the cabins — became inexpressibly vile. Washing, even if water could be spared, was difficult; the straw mattresses the passengers brought with them soon fell apart, drenched and rotten; passengers became too ill or too demoralised to clear up after themselves; and the water itself was frequently undrinkable. 'The *George Canning* . . . had two kinds of water for her passengers,' said the *New York Times* in 1853, after the ship in question arrived with a death-roll of eighteen passengers and a dying four-year-old child; 'fit, drinkable water for the captain, the cabin passengers and the crew; and bilge-water, or water taken from the ocean, for the steerage emigrants.' It was under conditions like these that over seven million people travelled to America in the first three-quarters of the nineteenth century; it was in conditions like these that the prudent passenger hoped to maintain his health and that of his family.

That the battle was very often a losing one is shown by the types of illness that flourished on the emigrant ships. A poster published by the Colonial Land and Emigrant Office begins: 'Cholera having made its appearance on board . . . '. Cholera is today defined as 'an acute epidemic infectious disease caused by a specific germ', and the most important method of transmission is by contaminated water; the disease is linked with overcrowding and dirt. Dysentery was extremely common. 'Epidemics', *Black's Medical Dictionary* goes on, 'are . . . encouraged by overcrowding and insanitary conditions. In the East, uncooked vegetables are a potent source of infection, as are cooks and other food-handlers who are carriers of the disease.' On the western ocean, the do-it-yourself cooks of the steerage were, of course, as likely to be infected as anyone else.

Then there was typhus, otherwise known as 'ship's fever'. In 1847, over 17,000 emigrants to Canada alone died from it either during or after the voyage. And, in common with all packet-ship emigrants, those who survived would have tales to tell of other, less insidious, abuses their bodies were made to suffer. The sailors behaved to their human cargo as they did to each other; cabin passengers might be sacrosanct, but the wretched steerage class was fair game and beaten up accordingly. Women had worse to fear, as is indicated by the provisions of an act pushed through Congress by popular request. This stipulated that any American sailor who used a promise of marriage, gifts, solicitation, threats, or 'the exercise of his authority' to seduce a passenger should marry her, pay up or go to prison. In case of danger, sailor brutality could on occasion assume an actively lethal form; survivors of shipwrecks had ugly stories to tell of how seamen would head the rush for the boats, and the devil take the hindmost.

Of Canada's typhus-ridden emigrant intake in 1847, three-quarters somehow managed to come through their ordeal by sea and to move on into the interior of the Promised Land. It is probable that, whatever happened to them subsequently, few would suffer in quite so uniquely terrible a fashion again. The little ships, though not killers in their own right, were deadly when their size was combined with human greed and human desperation.

'Row upon row of large hutches — hutches for humans'.

5. *Big Steam*

From the 1840s onwards, emigrants to America poured across the Atlantic in an unceasing flow. The age of mass travel — travel undertaken under the most wretched of conditions, but mass travel all the same — had suddenly arrived. The packet-rats, whose equally wretched existence made the whole phenomenon possible, watched events with a sardonic eye and made up songs about them. One of these, a windlass shanty now known as *We're All Bound to Go*, celebrated the vicious phonetic trick played by the ships' agents on the Irish: 'I've got the *Jinny Walker*,' says the unsuspecting heroine,

The *Singapore* carrying troops to the Cape in 1851 *en route* for Bombay.

Emigrants on deck in clear weather.

'and today she does set sail/With five and fifty emigrants and a thousand bags of meal.' The point was that, to Irish ears, the words *meal* and *mail* sounded pretty much the same; the hapless emigrant would jump to the conclusion that the leaking tub whose advantages were being pressed on him was a record-breaking packet, laden to the gunwale with transatlantic post.

The emigrants embarked in their thousands, suffered, survived or died — and the packet lines soared to the peak of their fortunes. Sail had never been so profitable and never would be again. The heyday of the Atlantic packets and the brief dazzle of the great cargo-clippers such as the *Ariel*, the *Taeping* and the *Cutty Sark* both represented the last flare-up of the candle before it went out for good. Within a few years, indeed, the *Jinny Walker* shanty would have a new verse that very definitely showed which way the wind was blowing. In the new version the heroine starts making plans for a trip home:

I'll go back on one of the White Star Lines, they carry both steam and sail,
And there I'll get plenty of beef and soft tack, and none of your yellow meal.

The message was clear: the two new forces of steam and mass travel had been linked. Terry Coleman, in his classic study of British and Irish emigrants, puts the date of the link-up in the mid-1850s: 'By 1855,' he writes, 'substantial numbers were travelling by steamship, and it was the steamship, and not the reforming, humanitarian or self-interested motives of any government, which made the Atlantic passage in steerage for the first time tolerable.' And the emigrants, in their turn, provided the market that was finally to free the ocean-going steamship from its early status of an experimental and ruinously expensive luxury.

Just how ruinous had already been demonstrated by two out of the three steam pioneers: the Great Western Company and Junius Smith's British and American Steam. The Smith enterprise went first. Despite passenger complaints about the food, the *British Queen*, when eventually she was launched, was a success; but shortly afterwards her sister ship *President* steamed out of New York into oblivion. Glossily new (she was only on her third round trip), laden with 136 passengers and crew and commanded by the same Dick Roberts who had taken the *Sirius* on her transatlantic race, she was last spotted tossing and pitching in a storm off the American coast. The observation was made by a sailing packet which finally reached Liverpool in safety; *President* was never seen again.

Remarking that it was 'virtually impossible' for any North Atlantic steamship to operate without a subsidy, the owners sold off the *British*

Deck of the *Great Eastern*.

Queen to Belgium (for whom she made a substantial loss) and went out of business.

The Great Western Company's failure was marked not so much by disgrace as by plain hard luck. The trouble was that, inspired by Brunel, the company thought big — and size that was not underwritten by profits brought the inevitable result. Faced with competition from the new Cunard line, Great Western decided to produce a ship that was not just faster and better but revolutionary. She was to be made of iron, not wood; she would be driven by a screw propeller, not paddles. She would be bigger than anything else afloat. And yet, when Brunel's *Great Britain* finally made her maiden voyage after six years in the shipyard (she was so big that she stuck in the dock's entrance, which had to be altered on the spot), she set off with only sixty passengers. She had been fitted out to take six times as many. The very next year, 1846, a multiplicity of factors, including faulty charts and the unforeseen effect of so much iron on her compass, sent her aground on what her captain thought was the Isle of Man. It turned out to be Dundrum Bay in Northern Ireland. Crew and passengers were all taken off, but the *Great Britain* stayed there for the winter, 'lying', as the desperate Brunel wrote to the Great Western's company secretary, 'like a useless saucepan kicking about on the most exposed shores that you can imagine'.

Despite the battering her iron hull received (and survived), the *Great Britain* had a far longer life than her corporate owners. She was

The launching of the *Great Britain* at Bristol.

Aboard a P & O steamer in the 1860s; note the game of quoits — and the dog.

salvaged, sold off, re-fitted and, after one transatlantic trip, went to work on a different emigrant run: the race for Australian gold. Compared with the passenger clippers, she was felt to be grubby but admirably well-behaved; she continued to behave well on that route for thirty years and still had further go in her. Finally, her engines were taken out, her masts and rigging for the first time began to do a full-time job, and — like the pioneering *Savannah* before her — she regressed to become an ordinary sailing-ship. Even when she sprang a leak off Cape Horn and was dumped in the windswept Falkland Islands, her life was not over. She lay there, a rusting, cannibalised hulk, for over eighty years, and then, in 1970, was rescued by British enthusiasts and towed back to her birthplace on the Avon, where she can be seen today. The *Great Britain* was a ship that wouldn't die.

Great Western Steam, however, sold the valiant *Great Western* in 1847 and wound up their whole business five years later. Of the Big Three companies in transatlantic steam, two were down with one still to go.

That one, however, was the British and North American Royal Mail Steam Packet Company, otherwise known as Cunard; and, where rivals got their sums wrong, buried themselves under ton-weights of

R.M.S. "BRITANNIA"

1840

THE CUNARD STEAM-SHIP COMPANY LIMITED.

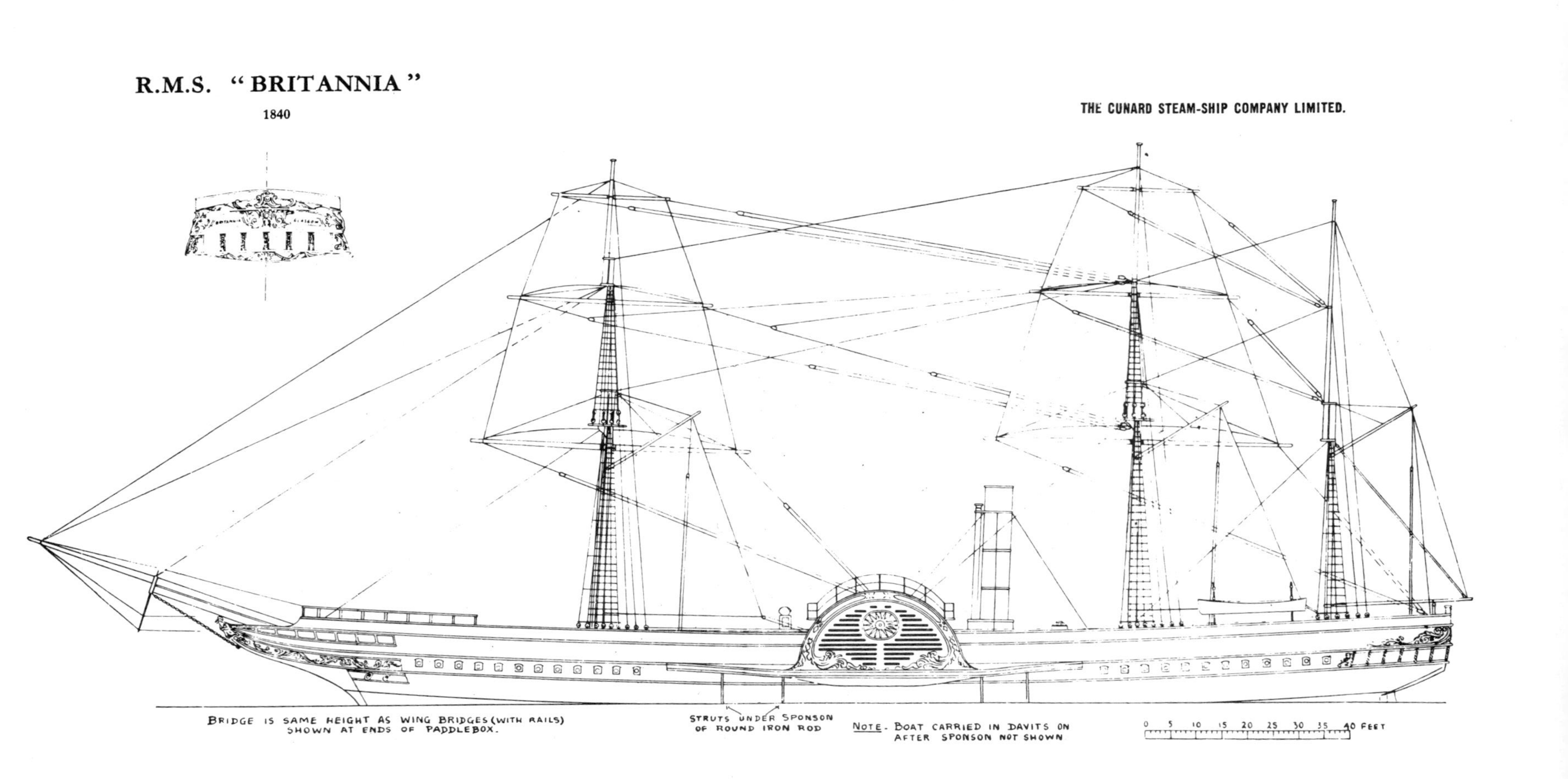

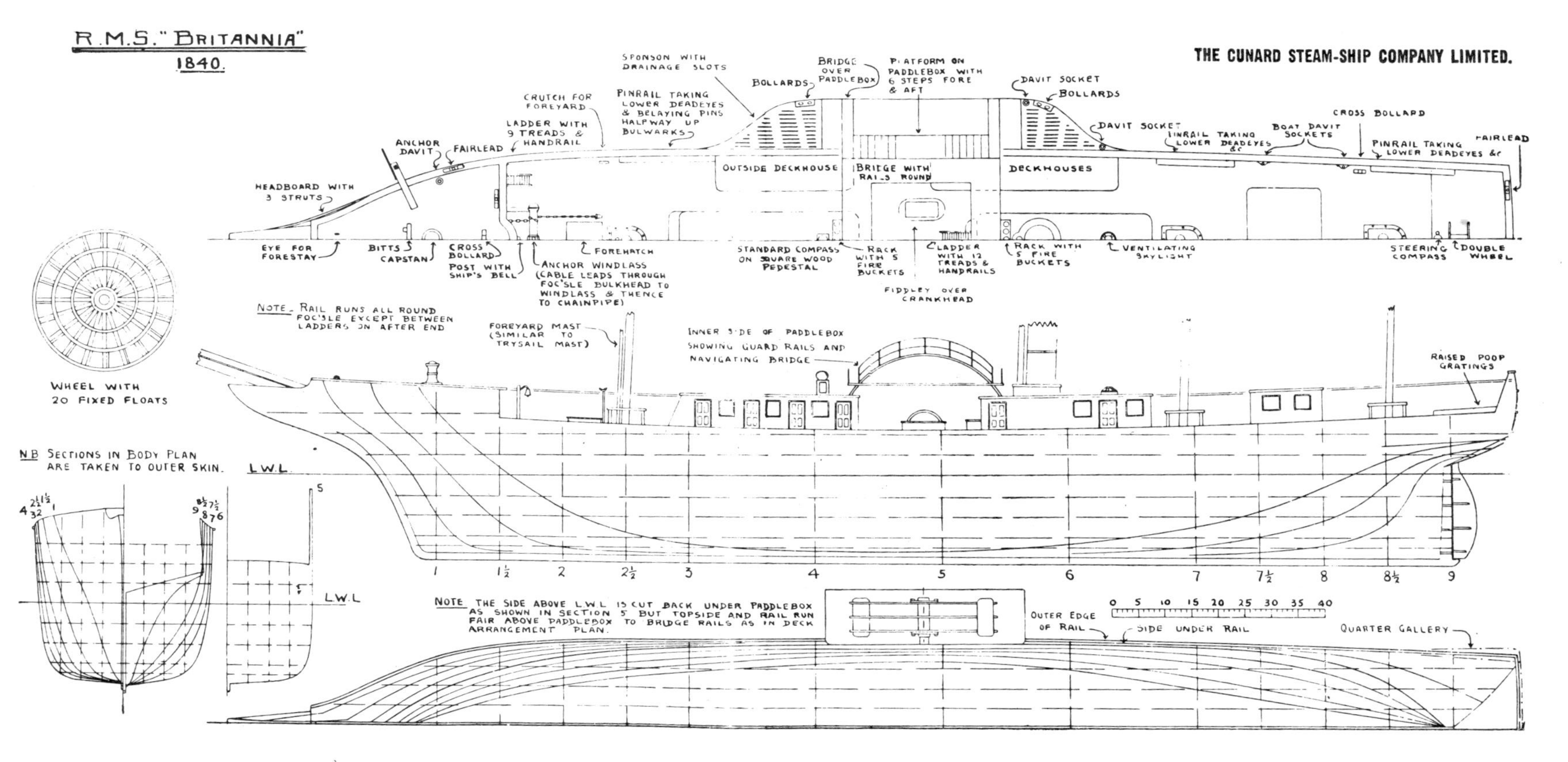
R.M.S. "BRITANNIA"
1840.
THE CUNARD STEAM-SHIP COMPANY LIMITED.
SPONSON WITH DRAINAGE SLOTS
BRIDGE OVER PADDLEBOX
PLATFORM ON PADDLEBOX WITH 6 STEPS FORE & AFT
BOLLARDS
DAVIT SOCKET
BOLLARDS
CRUTCH FOR FOREYARD
PINRAIL TAKING LOWER DEADEYES & BELAYING PINS HALFWAY UP BULWARKS
LADDER WITH 9 TREADS & HANDRAIL
ANCHOR DAVIT
FAIRLEAD
DAVIT SOCKET
PINRAIL TAKING LOWER DEADEYES &c
BOAT DAVIT SOCKETS
CROSS BOLLARD
PINRAIL TAKING LOWER DEADEYES &c
FAIRLEAD
HEADBOARD WITH 3 STRUTS
OUTSIDE DECKHOUSE
BRIDGE WITH RAILS ROUND
DECKHOUSES
EYE FOR FORESTAY
BITTS
CAPSTAN
CROSS BOLLARD
POST WITH SHIP'S BELL
FOREHATCH
ANCHOR WINDLASS (CABLE LEADS THROUGH FOC'SLE BULKHEAD TO WINDLASS & THENCE TO CHAINPIPE)
STANDARD COMPASS ON SQUARE WOOD PEDESTAL
RACK WITH 5 FIRE BUCKETS
LADDER WITH 12 TREADS & HANDRAILS
FIDDLEY OVER CRANKHEAD
RACK WITH 5 FIRE BUCKETS
VENTILATING SKYLIGHT
STEERING COMPASS
DOUBLE WHEEL
NOTE RAIL RUNS ALL ROUND FOC'SLE EXCEPT BETWEEN LADDERS ON AFTER END
FOREYARD MAST (SIMILAR TO TRYSAIL MAST)
INNER SIDE OF PADDLEBOX SHOWING GUARD RAILS AND NAVIGATING BRIDGE
RAISED POOP GRATINGS
WHEEL WITH 20 FIXED FLOATS
N.B SECTIONS IN BODY PLAN ARE TAKEN TO OUTER SKIN.
L.W.L.
L.W.L
1 1½ 2 2½ 3 4 5 6 7 7½ 8 8½ 9
NOTE THE SIDE ABOVE L.W.L IS CUT BACK UNDER PADDLEBOX AS SHOWN IN SECTION 5 BUT TOPSIDE AND RAIL RUN FAIR ABOVE PADDLEBOX TO BRIDGE RAILS AS IN DECK ARRANGEMENT PLAN.
0 5 10 15 20 25 30 35 40
OUTER EDGE OF RAIL
SIDE UNDER RAIL
QUARTER GALLERY

Passenger cabin in the 1860s.

debts and expensive fittings and collapsed, Cunard stayed firmly and obstinately viable. The company had, it is true, the all-important mail subsidy. But it also had a brilliant engineer and ship-builder, Robert Napier of Clydeside, and — in Samuel Cunard himself — a founder whose genius in the business of running ships equalled that of the great Brunel in building them.

Cunard's biggest breakthrough was a surprisingly simple one — but, if it had not been for the safety-net provided by the subsidy, it is questionable whether he could have pulled it off. In a period when an obsession with knots was the hallmark of all shipping firms, Cunard deliberately chose to stress safety rather than speed. As the firm's instructions to its captains were to say later: 'Your ship is loaded, take her; speed is nothing, follow your own road, deliver her safe, bring her back safe — safety is all that is required.' Indeed, Cunard flouted tradition still further; the *Great Western* might drip with luxury, the *Liverpool*'s interior might glow with silk hangings and rosewood, but the as yet unbuilt Cunarders were going to eschew such unnecessary frills in favour of profit. 'I want a plain and comfortable boat, not the least unnecessary expense for show,' Cunard directed when negotiations with Napier were opened. 'I prefer plain work in the cabin and it will save a large amount in the cost . . . .'

The first product of the 'plain and comfortable' policy was the paddle-steamer *Britannia*; 228 feet (or seven London buses) long, 34 feet broad; cabin-space for 124 passengers; a record-beater for speed (she once logged 280 miles in one day); and immortalised by Charles Dickens as the cause of his succinct self-diagnosis: 'Not ill, but going to be.'

Previous pages: elevation, plan and section from the *Britannia*, 1840.

Dickens crossed the Atlantic on the *Britannia* in January 1842. Like many others after him, he was going on a lecture tour of the United States — and, when the time came to return, he went back by sailing packet. As far as the *Britannia* was concerned, he'd had enough.

To be fair, the weather had been appalling, and the journey lasted an anything but record-breaking eighteen days. The cook got drunk; the boat squawked, groaned and creaked 'like an enormous fire of the driest possible twigs'; one lifeboat was smashed, as were the boxes enclosing the paddles; the fire in the main cabin was out more often than not. Mrs Dickens, her maid and Dickens himself were all prostrated with sea-sickness, though they later recovered enough to deal with menus that included 'a steaming dish of baked potatoes, and another of roasted apples; and plates of pig's face, cold ham, salt beef; or perhaps a smoking mess of rare hot collops'. (In fact, baked potatoes, roast apples and ham are probably the best dishes possible for tempting a queasy stomach.) Dickens and his wife ate with gusto. But the accommodation that his £40 ticket bought him did nothing to alleviate his discomfort.

In the saloon, 'plain and comfortable' meant this:

> Before descending into the bowels of the ship, we had passed from the deck into a long narrow apartment, not unlike a gigantic hearse with windows in the sides; having at the upper end a melancholy stove, at which three or four chilly stewards

Embarkation scene, late nineteenth century.

were warming their hands; while on either side, extending down its whole dreary length, was a long, long table, over each of which a rack, fixed to the low roof, and stuck full of drinking-glasses and cruet-stands, hinted dismally at rolling seas and heavy weather.

The cabin was plainer still:

That this state-room had been specially engaged for 'Charles Dickens, Esquire, and Lady' was rendered sufficiently clear even to my scared intellect by a very small manuscript announcing the fact which was pinned on a very flat quilt, covering a very thin mattress, spread like a surgical plaster on a most inaccessible shelf.

A sketch made at the time shows that, however much Dickens loved wordsmithing, he was deadly accurate on the essentials; two bunks, with curtains and 'very flat' coverings; twin washbowls (no running water, of course); a small mirror, a water-flask and two glasses; three coat-hooks; a hard-looking settee (Dickens called it a 'horsehair perch'); and a lamp. The only real concession to comfort, as modern travellers would understand it, was the provision of a small railing fixed to the wall beside each pillow. However incapacitated or comatose, passengers would have something to hang on to as the ship pitched and rolled.

Spartan, though ready-furnished, state-rooms; a long, functional saloon mostly taken up by table; questionable heating arrangements

On board P & O's *Ceylon*, 1881: views of the dining saloon, the ladies' boudoir and the deck.

Red Sea afternoon on the P & O *Venetia*.

(none, naturally, in the cabin); and — the bright spot — reasonable food: Dickens might already have been on the sailing-packet he decided to go home in. However, the mail-carrying *Britannia* and her sister ships *Caledonia*, *Acadia* and *Columbia* could boast far greater averages in speed and regularity than even the fastest packets, while their 'safety is all' motto was vindicated when the *Columbia* was wrecked without the loss of a single life. A ship that, however plain, offered a twelve- or fourteen-day passage from England to Boston was definitely a commercial attraction, and travellers with the money to spare began to take advantage of it. The Bostonians thought highly of it, too; when Boston harbour froze over in the worst winter for fifty years and sealed the *Britannia* in, city worthies raised $1500 on the spot for a canal to be cut through the ice. Whatever happened, the *Britannia* had to maintain her sailing schedule. In fact, she left only two days late; there was delighted comment on the 'spectacle of an ocean steamer moving down the harbour accompanied by thousands of

1. A distinguished passenger: Gen. Sir F. Roberts.
2. Our Captain, P. and O. C^o. Steamer "Paramatta"
3. Passengers on the look-out, in the Suez Canal.
4. Afternoon tea-party in the Red Sea.
5. A perplexed lottery manager.
6. In the music room.
7. Summer and Winter.

The Cock fighting game.
The water jump in the shipboard obstacle race.

Opposite: P & O impressions.

people running or skating by her side'. Unthreatened by serious Atlantic competitors, the subsidised Cunard quickly established a lead in Big Steam that looked all but impossible to challenge.

All the same, there was clearly room for competition. The first to try it on a grand scale was a sailing-packet magnate, Edward Knight Collins of the American Dramatic Line, and the angle he took on the question was characteristic. Let the British Cunarders be as dowdy as they liked; *his* new enterprise would go for the old packet virtues of dash, speed and glamour. Especially glamour; as far as physical luxury went, the sailing ships were necessarily circumscribed, but there seemed no limit to what could be achieved on considerably larger vessels. In addition, Collins had done a 'Cunard' on his own account: the United States government, smarting at the way a British firm had swiped the top end of the shipping market, awarded the Yankee ship-owner an annual mail subsidy of $385,000 in return for a promised twenty trips a year between Liverpool and New York.

The new company set to work and came up with four sister ships that fully restored the ideal of luxury to the transatlantic run. The *Atlantic*, the *Pacific*, the *Arctic* and the *Baltic* were as plush as their designers could make them. The *Atlantic* had mirrors, rosewood panels and coloured windows galore; there was an unheard-of innovation, steam-heating, and two more in the shape of bathrooms (baths in pre-Collins days were taken on deck, at the working end of a hosepipe) and a barber's shop. There was a cold compartment, large enough to take forty tons of ice, and a smoking-room; there was real marble on the state-room tables and real green peas on the menu. This last was, indeed, mouth-watering by the standards of any period: turtle soup; boiled turkey with oyster sauce; roast beef, veal, lamb, goose, duck, fowl; filet de pigeon au Cronstaugh; Salmi de canard sauvage; green corn; currant tartlets; apple tart; fruit, nuts, olives; coffee and lemonade (frozen). There were only two blots on the scene: the state rooms were designed — and charged — for two, which annoyed single passengers; and the tightly-stuffed, shiny seats so beloved by earlier shipping lines were still present. As on the *Britannia*, and on the packets before her, passengers sitting at table were liable to vanish under it during a sudden swell.

Within two years of the *Atlantic*'s mid-century maiden voyage, Collins had grabbed 50 per cent more first-class passengers than Cunard. The *Atlantic* captured speed records, too: ten days, sixteen hours; nine days, twenty hours; nine days, eighteen hours. But the winning, time after time, of the prized Blue Riband of the Atlantic was achieved only at stupendous expense in terms of mechanical wear and tear. Observing this, Cunard kept its corporate cool, although there is a faint element of whistling to keep spirits up in the Cunard manager's

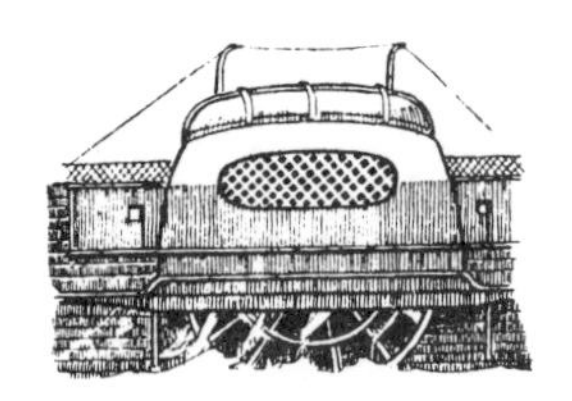

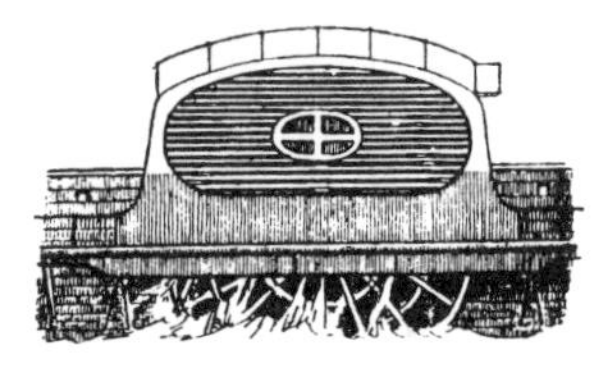

Paddle-boxes: from top to bottom, *Avon* (1841); *Orinoco* (1851); *Solent* (1853).

remark that Collins was 'finding that breaking our windows with sovereigns, though very fine fun, is too costly to keep up'.

As things turned out, however, he was right — and tragically so. Within two years of its beginnings, the Collins company seemed all set for victory; within seven, the company was bankrupt, two of its ships at the bottom of the ocean and its founder three times bereaved. When, in 1854, the fog-bound *Arctic* rammed the much smaller French steamer *Vesta* and sank, Collins's wife, son and only daughter were among the 322 people on her who drowned. The details were savagely ironic; when the *Vesta* was hit, some of her passengers and crew rushed to the boats with the idea of reaching safety on the vessel that had rammed them. The two lifeboats they occupied were both swamped — but the *Vesta*, damaged though she was, managed to limp home. The *Arctic*, meanwhile, was also convinced that her victim was in deadly danger, and a boat was sent off through the fog to the rescue. But it was the *Arctic* herself that needed rescuing: with three gaping holes in her hull, she sank in four hours. Two boats finally made it to safety, as did a makeshift raft; this last, when spotted by another ship, was occupied by just one of the seventy-six people who had scrambled on to it. In the fifteen hours that had elapsed since the *Arctic* went down, the other seventy-five had died of exposure or been swept into the sea.

The same year saw another shipping disaster of even greater magnitude: the iron-hulled, screw-propelled *City of Glasgow*, carrying 480 souls, steamed out of Liverpool and vanished. But, unlike Collins's company, the *City of Glasgow*'s owners, the Inman Line, survived. The reason was that founder William Inman had developed a completely different approach to the passenger shipping business, one that was finally to make it independent of subsidies, hand-outs and the like. He, too, went back to the packet-ships for inspiration, but in a quite different way from his luckless American competitor: he discovered the paying power of the emigrant.

Both Cunard and Collins aimed at the luxury market and charged accordingly; Inman chopped his first- and second-class fares and introduced a steerage rate of eight guineas a head, *with food*. Since an emigrant could find himself paying that much for a sailing ship passage, the bargain was an excellent one; from then on, the packet's supremacy was shot to pieces.

In addition, Inman arranged for his ships to call at the Irish port of Queenstown (now Cork). On one occasion, he and his wife made the Liverpool to Queenstown trip themselves as steerage passengers, to check that conditions were as they should be. The changes these conditions represented were, by the standards of the times, almost revolutionary. For his eight guineas, the Inman Line emigrant got washing facilities (with clean towel, soap and mirror); a numbered berth, with separate compartments for women; and a bill of fare that, while unexciting, offered good solid stuff — coffee, fresh bread, porridge, beef, fish, and plum-pudding on Sunday.

Equally dramatic changes were pioneered in the design of the ships themselves. After the *Great Britain* — a one-off job anyway, though a brilliant one — the *City of Glasgow* was the first transatlantic steamer of importance to flout the die-hards who said that iron couldn't float and that a screw propellor at the stern would hinder steering. (The die-hards, of course, were numerous — 'contrary to nature' was the comment of one anti-iron man.) But there was no altering the statistics. Compared with the *Asia*, a wooden paddler of the Cunard line, the *City of Glasgow* burned only a quarter as much coal a day, could take on between two and three times as much cargo and had accommodation for 537 passengers as opposed to 160. Suddenly, ocean passages under steam stopped being a dodgy commercial venture, and the Atlantic — until then ruled by Cunard, its fleeting competitors and the sailing ships — became a businessman's free-for-all. So, for the first time, did the other big emigrant run: the passage to Australia.

The second *Orinoco* of the Royal Mail Line, 1886.

From a steamship line's point of view, the western ocean, though it could be fiendish in its weather conditions, was a comparatively straightforward nut to crack, but the London to Melbourne route was very much harder. This was the clippers' preserve; no steamer, unless it was prepared to make full use of its sails, could carry enough coal for anything like the whole run, so stops at bunkering ports were essential and frequent. But bunkering arrangements were a major headache, and the overheads soared yearly. In the 1850s, for example, P & O employed 170 sailing ships just to get the coal out to where the company's steamers would pick it up.

Could the new type of ship offer any worthwhile competition? Several firms, including Cunard, decided to have a go. The result, in most cases, was the same: it was no good. The great Brunel came up

Peninsular Steam Navigation Company.

TAGUS, of 800 Tons and 300 Horse Power.
ROYAL TAR, of 650 Tons and 264 Horse Power.
BRAGANZA, of 650 Tons and 264 Horse Power.
IBERIA, of 600 Tons and 200 Horse Power.
LIVERPOOL, of 500 Tons and 160 Horse Power.

BRANCH VESSELS.

PENINSULA, plies between Cadiz & Seville.
GUADALQUIVER, to ply between San Lucar & Seville.
ESTRELLA, and SOL, } plying between Cadiz, San Mary's, & Port Royal.

The "Royal Tar"

Commander,

Will start from off Blackwall, on Friday the 7 June } 1839
at 9 o'Clock Am and from Falmouth, on MONDAY, 10 Do

WITH HER MAJESTY'S MAILS,

In charge of ***Admiralty Agent,***

For VIGO, LISBON, CADIZ, And Gibraltar,

CALLING OFF OPORTO, weather permitting, (and the Oporto Mails not having been landed at Vigo,) **returning by the same Route.**

The Rates of Fare will include a Table, &c. as per Regulations exhibited in the Cabins, and which may also be seen at the Offices.

RATES OF FARE.

		First Cabin.		Second Cabin.
Vigo, Oporto, and Lisbon	From or to London....	£17 0 0	—	£11 10 0
	From or to Falmouth ..	15 0 0	—	9 10 0
Cadiz and Gibraltar	From or to London....	20 0 0	—	14 0 0
	From or to Falmouth ..	18 0 0	—	12 0 0

Intermediate Distances. *(Provisions included.)*

		1st Cabin.	2nd Cabin.	Deck.
Vigo to	Oporto	7 doll...	5 doll...	2 dollars.
	Lisbon	20	,, ..10	,, .. 5 ,,
	Cadiz or Gibraltar	40	,, ..25	,, ..10 ,,
		Mill. Reis.	Mill. Reis.	Mill. Reis
Lisbon to Vigo......		18 500 ..	9 500 ..	4 800
Oporto to Vigo......		7 400 ..	4 700 ..	1 900

	1st Cabin. Mill. Reis.	2nd Cabin. Mill. Reis.	Deck. Mill. Reis.
From Oporto to Lisbon......	14 400....	11 000....	4 800
From Lisbon to Cadiz	20 400....	13 000....	4 800
From Lisbon to Gibraltar	26 000....	17 000....	6 000
From Cadiz to Gibraltar	8 dollars..	5 dollars.	. 3 doll.
From Cadiz to Lisbon	21 ,,	..15 ,,	.. 7 ,,
From Gibraltar to Lisbon....	29 ,,	..20 ,,	..10 ,,
From Gibraltar to Cadiz	8 ,,	.. 5 ,,	.. 3 ,,

Children of Passengers under Three Years of Age to go free; under Ten Years of Age, to pay as Second Cabin Passengers; and above Ten, as Cabin Passengers.

Passengers not proceeding after taking their Passage, to forfeit Half the Passage Money.

The *Royal Tar* at sea.

with what he surely felt must be the answer — a huge ship, six times the size of anything else in the seas, capable of sailing to the Indian sub-continent without stopping — but even this would not do. The ship — the extraordinary *Great Eastern* — was built; Brunel, exhausted by the herculean venture, collapsed on board the day before her maiden voyage and died a week later; and, for some inscrutable reason, the owners put the iron marvel, with its accommodation for 4000 passengers and bunkers for 10,000 tons of coal, to join the run-of-the-mill steamer trade from Liverpool to New York. She carried on until 1888, when she was sold for scrap. Her only moments of glory were when, transformed into a cable ship, she laid the first (and, later, three more) transatlantic cables. Even during her lifetime, she was regarded as worse than unlucky; she was somehow frightening. The horrible rumour grew up that her double bottom contained the bodies of two riveters who had accidentally been walled up alive. She was an ace of spades among ships.

The problem of the Australia run was finally solved by the introduction of the compound engine. This, an offshoot of mining engineering (and a fifty-year-old one; the maritime diehards had been at work again), allowed the power of one 'batch' of steam to be used several times. The savings involved are obvious — and they were immediately pounced upon by the P & O, the liners working the Pacific and yet another arrival on the Atlantic scene: the White Star Line. This, by far the most dangerous rival Cunard had to face, followed the well-established pattern of carrying three classes of passengers, but it combined this with outdoing anything the ill-fated Collins line had ever attempted. For all that — like their contemporaries — the White Star ships still carried sails, they looked different, felt different and even sounded different. They were not merely the ancestors but the parents of the ocean-going liner of today.

Opposite: the beginnings of the P & O. The poster announces one of the early sailings of the Peninsular Steam Navigation Company's *Royal Tar*; note the fares.

Dinner call for first-class passengers.

6. *The Palace and the Iceberg*

In August 1870 — when women wore bustles and bonnets, when Europe was embroiled in the Franco-Prussian War and when Queen Victoria still had thirty years to live — the first of the White Star liners splashed off a Belfast slipway and floated. Forty-one years and many White Star launchings later — at a time when women wore hobble skirts and hats like wash-basins, when experts could hear the rumblings of another European war and when George V was King-Emperor — another steamer of the line was officially christened. The first of these two ships set a pattern of White Star nomenclature that would last sixty years; it was called the *Oceanic*. The second — carrying on the *ic* suffix — was named *Titanic*.

Two ships, divided by nearly half a century, by giant strides in technology and by their ultimate reputations. The *Oceanic* had berths for 1200 passengers all told; the *Titanic* could carry 2603 — and, if she had met her end later in her career, would probably have had that number on board when she did so. The *Oceanic*'s maximum speed was in the region of twelve knots; the *Titanic* was doing twenty-two knots when she hit the iceberg that was to kill her. The *Oceanic* had one stubby funnel and also carried four iron masts; the *Titanic*'s four-funnelled profile was to etch itself indelibly on the minds of all those who watched her sink.

Yet there were similarities that, given hindsight, make it possible to trace the factors leading to the *Titanic*'s fate from their earliest beginnings. In a sense, it was pure random chance that picked out this particular ship for disaster; given the trends and circumstances that brought her into existence, that same disaster could have overtaken any one of half-a-dozen others. It just happened to be the White Star's *Titanic* that proved beyond all shadow of doubt that — however much it is shut away behind steel, gilded wood, mirrors and potted palms — the sea remains a potential killer.

This was something that, in earlier days, no ocean voyager was able for even an instant to forget. The relationship between the sea and the light wooden vessels that crossed it was an intimate one, and every

A club . . . or a ship? A passengers' smoking room in the late nineteenth century.

detail of the sea's behaviour was instantly obvious to all aboard. In 1842, Mrs Dickens and her maid went into 'ecstasies of fear' when the *Britannia* shipped an extra-heavy wave — and no wonder. The water, her husband wrote, 'forced its way through the skylights, burst open the doors above, and came raging and roaring down into the ladies' cabin'. Dickens also pointed out that a bad winter's night on the Atlantic was impossible to imagine or describe.

> To say that (the ship) is flung down on her side in the waves, with her masts dipping into them, and that, springing up again, she rolls over on the other side, until a heavy sea strikes her with the noise of a hundred great guns, and hurls her back — that she stops, staggers and shivers, as though stunned, and then, with a violent throbbing at her heart, darts onward like a monster goaded into madness, to be beaten down, and battered, and crushed, and leaped on by the angry sea — that thunder, lightning, hail, and rain, and wind, are all in fierce contention for the mastery — that every plank has its groan, every nail its shriek, and every drop of water in the great ocean its howling voice — is nothing . . . Only a dream can call it up again.

The changeover from wood to iron and from paddles to screws made ships tougher, faster and immensely more efficient as passenger-carriers. But the enemy was still recognisable and recognised. In 1856, the steam-and-sail ship *Royal Charter*, carrying a full load of passengers and half a million pounds in gold, sailed from Melbourne in August, made a fast and unscathed passage round the notorious Cape Horn, set a fast clip up through the southern Atlantic — and broke up in a Force 12 October storm off the Anglesey shore. On the Beaufort Scale, Force 12 is a hurricane. 'In that gale', K. C. Barnaby, the naval architect, writes in his history of ship disasters, 'only a modern ocean-going

The Red Sea: the ladies lie down after lunch.

salvage tug would have had the slightest chance of bringing the *Royal Charter* away from that menacing lee shore . . . . No lifeboats could have been launched.' Only thirty-four out of her complement of nearly 500 got ashore; the gold also went to the bottom.

It was a freak storm that finished the *Royal Charter*. Other ships of the period that foundered in less heavy weather did so because of design faults — faults that, once recognised, were corrected. That they tended to be corrected slowly was a result, in part at least, of plain short-sighted greed. The sail-and-steam clipper *London*, which also worked the England-Australia run and sank in 1866 in the Bay of Biscay, did so basically because she sat too deep in the water. 'Ship too heavily laden for its size and too crank' read a bottle-message washed ashore later on the French coast. 'Windows stove in and water coming in everywhere. Storm not too bad for a ship in good condition. Shipped such heavy seas that engine-room hatchway carried away and extinguished fires so that no pumps available.' Survivors — three passengers and sixteen crew members who lived through twenty hours of storm conditions in an open boat — clothed this pathetically concise account with further details. The bad weather which had pursued the *London* from England had finally carried off her rigging and one of the lifeboats. The ship's innards had been gashed open by a 'mountain of water' that had torn away the engine-room casing and hatchway. The furnaces had been flooded in ten minutes. The crew and passengers had struggled with the deck pumps in vain. No rafts could be constructed since the *London*'s mainmast and spars — the traditional source of raft material — were made of iron. The captain, urging his chief engineer to take charge of the group that was later rescued, had said: 'There is not much chance for this boat. There is none for the ship. Your duty is done, mine is to remain here. Get in and take command of the few it will hold.' The news of the loss of the *London* brought an immediate change in the pattern of ship construction — from then onwards, engine-room hatches were built higher — and helped to cause a much more delayed one. Eleven years later, after further sinkings had fanned the protests, load-line marks became compulsory as a result of the campaign led by Samuel Plimsoll.

Until disaster proved them wrong, however, mistakes made by nineteenth-century ship designers were to some extent excusable. The notion of steam power was still a new one; the hidden strengths and weaknesses of building materials, of engines and of one type of design as against another were still being discovered by what was basically a process of on-the-job trial and error. But trial and error is one thing, crass idiocy another. The worst sea disaster of the whole century was caused by actions so startlingly idiotic as to imply that their perpetrators were already — despite continuing evidence to the contrary — succumbing to the fatal conclusion that the sea had been tamed.

At three o'clock in the morning of 1 April 1873, in clear weather, the transatlantic liner *Atlantic* came pounding up under full steam to the rocks of the Nova Scotia coast and rammed straight into them.

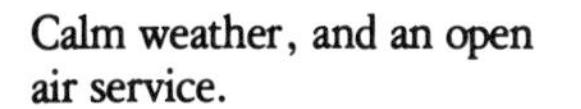

Calm weather, and an open air service.

Dressing for dinner.

Slowed down during the crossing by bad weather conditions, she had come close to running out of coal; the captain — who was asleep at the time of the collision — had decided to make for Halifax instead of New York. Two hundred passengers and crew members scrambled and swung ashore by means of five lifelines between the ship and the nearest rock; two hundred others somehow survived the night. The others — a total of 481 — drowned or died of exposure. 'It is a curious circumstance', said a contemporary writer, 'that not one female was saved. The women proved unable to bear the severe cold, the exhaustion and the terror; and many were frozen as they clung helplessly to the rigging, or lost their presence of mind as they attempted the passage from the ship to the rock.'

As her name implies, the *Atlantic* was a White Star ship, the twin sister, in fact, of the *Oceanic*. Within three years, their pioneering owners had both changed the face of sea-travel and provided it with its worst calamity to date. That there had been a change was well established by the time the *Atlantic* made her last crossing; indeed, the direction it would take was obvious to anyone who had bought a ticket for the *Oceanic*'s maiden voyage. True to current form, the *Oceanic* had provision for both sail and steam; but she also had open

Deckboard conversation.

railings rather than bulwarks, a promenade deck, a straight stem, a grand saloon sited amidships that stretched from one side of the vessel to the other, and a near 1:1 ratio of portholes to cabins. These, too, were placed amidships; White Star passengers could say goodbye to the noise and motion that hitherto had prostrated first-class passengers in their choice stern staterooms. Innovation was piled on luxurious innovation; in the cabins there was running water, an electric bell, steam heating, adjustable oil-lamps (two later White Star liners even experimented with gaslight, but the ship's movements caused the gas pipes to crack). There were more lavatories than anyone was used to; there were bathtubs. The shiny stuffed dining-room benches had disappeared; instead, each diner had an armchair to himself, which heartened those who dreaded the embarrassing onset of seasickness. No longer would there be a furtive competition for the end-of-the-bench seats.

White Star became positively lyrical over its inventions: 'Like the elephant that picks up a needle and tears down a tree, there is no task too small, no work too great for the giant, Steam. He warms the child's berth; he weighs the anchor; he turns the barber's brush; he loads and discharges the ship; and rests not night nor day.' And, despite the loss of the *Atlantic*, the passengers responded in like manner. The six great *-ic*s were both fast and gloriously comfortable. Cunard and the White Star's other competitors were left practically standing. Further refinements — cabin ventilation, electric lighting — speedily appeared, and popularity polls began to be held on the merits of the various captains. Some were jolly, some were gallant, some were staunch silent characters, and some were downright surly. Two of the Cunarder masters were surly types — yet another tiny item to be counted against the 'Safety First' line. Cunard might be safe, but the paying public wanted splendour — and they got it with White Star. One passenger used a phrase that was to become famous when he said

A visit to the engine room.

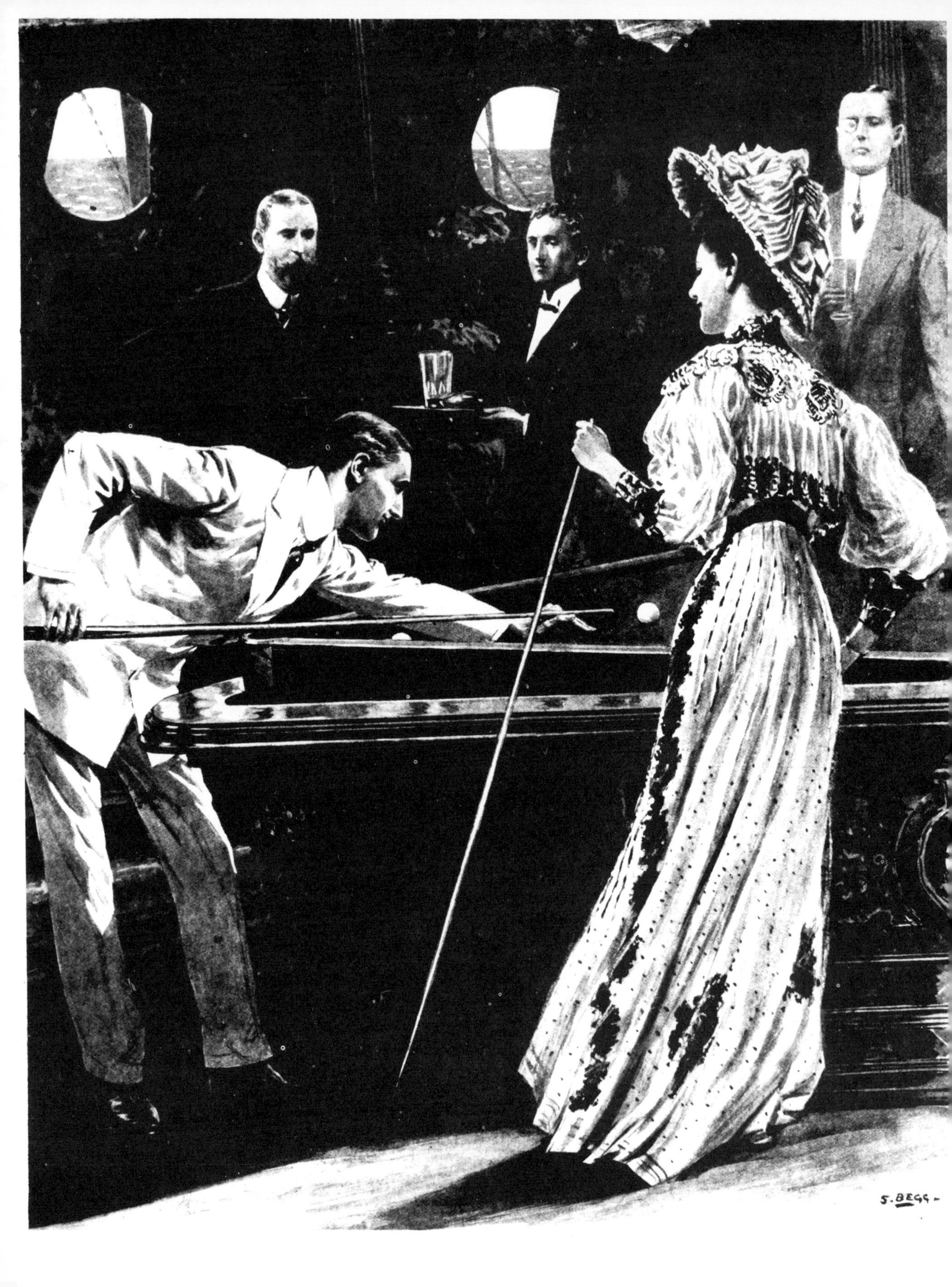
S. BEGG

Opposite: billiards in progress, on a self-levelling table.

of the *Republic* that it was 'a floating palace, with the style and comfort of a Swiss hotel. I am ready', he went on, 'to despair of finding any vessel more completely to my mind.' Not Dickens's mad monster, but a snug, soft drawing-room. In retrospect, the latter's connotations were to seem ominous.

Even Cunard, though, could not avoid being drawn into the desperate tussle that ensued for Atlantic mastery, especially since the other existing shipping lines had themselves joined the battle. By now, there were several of them: the Belgian White Cross Line; the German Norddeutsche Lloyd, Adler and Hapag (Hapag stood for the Hamburg Amerikanische Paketfahrtaktiengesellschaft); the Dutch Line Holland-America; the American Steamship Company. Equally strong competition was mounted by the three other main British companies in the field: the British Anchor, whose ships criss-crossed between Glasgow and New York every other week, and whose liner *Dido* was to be the first British steamer through the Suez Canal; the Liverpool and Great Western, usually called Guion after its American founder; and Inman, who had discovered the possibilities of the emigrant trade. Inman's particular reaction to the new Great Race was to launch the *City of Berlin*, a ship bigger than anything except the *Great Eastern* and one that proceeded to set a new westbound Atlantic record of under eight days. The *Berlin* had running water as a matter of course, and marble washtubs too; bath-times were arranged in advance with the steward, and the bath rota was written up on a slate outside each bathroom. Scope for exercise was also plentiful. 'You can have a promenade of nearly five hundred feet straight ahead,' commented a member of the *Berlin*'s passenger-list; 'the lower deck looks like a little town, and it is a great deal pleasanter than most little towns.' The ladies' public

Cricket on deck.

Dinner in rough weather.

room, the smoking-room and the officers' rooms resembled 'handsome-looking houses' on the ship's main street; all of them opened on to the deck on both sides.

Clearly, it was no time for Cunard to dally about. The firm's founder had died in 1865. The company went public and wiped the White Star's eye by producing something that could carry twice as many first-class passengers as her rivals' ships. Compared with these, the *Servia* was not particularly fast, but she captured the public's imagination in other ways: she had electric light throughout, five decks, patent lavatories attached to some of the cabins. And she was built of steel instead of iron. Another technological revolution had overtaken the passenger-ship trade.

True to the Cunard image, the *Servia* was not flashy — but she was dignified, restful, spacious and extremely popular. The line's fortunes bounced back again; three more *-ia*s came splashing down the slipways, and all three followed the *Servia*'s example of catering for passenger comfort as well as passenger anxiety. The *Aurania* — the *Servia*'s sister — was built wider in the beam so as to give greater stability; the *Umbria* had the first refrigerating machinery seen on a transatlantic liner; the *Etruria* had pipe organs in the music-rooms, cabins that could be booked *en suite* for travelling notables, and thirteen marble bathrooms with steam and shower apparatus. (The two latter ships were

Ship's galley.

also soon to enjoy another claim to fame that, while much more important, was also far less glorious; auxiliary sails were then on the way out, and when the two ships, one after the other, broke down in the middle of the Atlantic they had to stay there until rescued. In the case of the *Umbria*, her propeller-shaft fractured; the *Etruria*'s propeller simply dropped off. Clearly, trusting in the power of a single screw was like putting all your eggs in one basket; from then on, twin-screw ships were *de rigueur*.) And Cunard, by now as totally involved in the race as anyone, didn't stop there. The line's next offerings were two vast beauties called the *Campania* and the *Lucania*. In 1893, they were the largest ships in the world and, according to *The Times*, stood higher from the keel than the Eddystone Lighthouse and had funnels so large that a mail coach could have been driven through them 'as if through a tunnel'. Between them, they would turn the Atlantic crossing into a five-day affair and pioneer another major technical breakthrough. Late in her career, the *Lucania* carried the first radio installation capable of keeping in simultaneous touch with Europe and America. A modern globe-trotter, suddenly dumped on the *Campania*'s boat-deck, would notice only a faint general tinge of old-fashionedness: brass bedsteads in the first-class, an open firegrate in the smoking-room, iron portable berths in the steerage. Otherwise, with her huge dining-room, her geraniums in the ladies' boudoirs, velvet settees, grand

The butcher's shop.

pianos (replaced in the second-class drawing-room by a cottage one), the ship exactly resembled the sort of good, solid hotel that can still be found today in spas and cathedral towns. It was, of course, meant to: shutting out the sea was part of the idea. An even more ominous quotation than that about the 'floating palace' comes from a Cunard brochure, which pointed out that those rich enough to pay $600 a day for the privilege might spend their time on board 'seeing nothing at all that has to do with a ship, not even the sea'.

By the end of the century, ocean passages in general, and in particular the passage to America, had completely lost their 'do-or-die' image. Businessmen investigating new markets, lecturers following in Dickens's wake (their number included Oscar Wilde; 'I wish', said the captain in question afterwards, 'I had that man lashed to the bowsprit on the windward side') — for all of them the journey was now no longer a nightmare experience but something very nearly approaching a holiday. The still-increasing flood of emigrants, too, could now travel in conditions that, while very much 'below stairs' in

The shipboard game of buckets.

quality, were incomparably better than those of fifty years before. Their worst ordeals, in fact, were now bureaucratic in origin; the United States authorities, deeply embarrassed by the number of those yearning to be free who had taken up the invitation, had started prohibiting entry to anyone unlikely to be able to pay his way in the New World. The shipping lines became viciously selective as to whom they would take on board; the lunatic, the sick, the handicapped and the elderly were all rejected, as were unsupported women with children. Emigrants were no longer treated exactly like cattle, but they were still regarded as such.

Shipboard life was still strictly organised according to the social rules of the day; the second-class, composed of 'ladies and gentlemen', had their cottage piano and china plates, while the steerage, consisting of 'males and females', ate off tin dishes and had to bring their own concertinas or mouth-organs if they wanted music. The glowing splendours described in company brochures were, of course, mainly reserved for the top fee-payers, among whom an Atlantic voyage was

Cover of a 1925 edition of the White Star Line's house magazine.

rapidly becoming as much a matter of fashion as of necessity. You took the waters in Europe, admired London, bought dresses in Paris and wound up your vacation with five days on the most modish liner available.

'Vacationing' was a habit that spread. In ships such as the *Campania*, a new category of passenger had been added to the others: the traveller of only moderate means but boundless enthusiasm for travelling. For him, the goals were the Uffizi, St Peter's and Goethe's birthplace; to reach them, so a New England travel agent alleged, nothing was needed but a hundred dollars and a bike.

For potential clients, the same travel agent made up a 'shopping list' which outlines with startling frankness what travelling steerage was still all about.

Go first and buy a bottle or two of coffee essence, some lump sugar, and a couple of cans of condensed milk. Get a couple of bottles of pickles. Bring your own towels and a cake of soap. Bring a pillow, then get a camp stool or a cheap steamer's chair. It will not cost much and you can leave it at Southampton till you return. Sitting accommodation is always bad and hard to be got in steerage.

When you get your ticket stamped in the office at the head of the wharf and are at last on deck, scuttle down into the steerage hold, and throw your satchel into the vacant top bunk, as near the middle of the vessel as possible, and stay by it until the bunks are all taken up. You will find a clean coloured blanket in your bunk and a straw mattress. There will probably be twenty bunks in your compartment, and you will find that the stewards have put all English-speaking people together. They will be all single men where you are; married couples and children in the other side, and further from you, where you will not be allowed to go, the single women.

You will find in your bunk a large black tin cup, a deep soup plate, with 'Cunard Line' stamped on its white surface, a knife, fork and large spoon, all of which you are expected to keep clean yourself. This will be your bill of fare: beef soup or pea soup, with a scrap or two of meat in your plate, a tin of coffee, and plenty of very good bread and butter, breakfast, at eight o' clock; at eleven, your tin full of nice beef soup, plenty of beef, very good, but nearly always fresh, and potatoes; at supper, five o'clock, bread, butter and tea. On Friday you will have soup in the morning, but no meat, and fish at dinner; you will have pudding at Sunday's dinner, and a little marmalade once or twice in the evening. You will find everything scrupulously neat on board, and try to help that thing by keeping your bunk and your dishes neat. Keep a watch, too, on fellows who will try to steal your clean dishes and leave their dirty ones in place of yours; that is about the only kind of stealing you need fear . . .

Floating palaces for the rich; floating working-men's hostels for the poor — that, as the present century began, was the regular pattern of travelling by sea. The business had come a long way in a very short time, and the shipping companies were determined that it was to go further even faster. Three years before the old century closed, the German Norddeutsche Lloyd line jolted its competitors rigid by launching a super-liner, *Kaiser Wilhelm der Grosse*, named after the German Emperor. The *Kaiser Wilhelm* broke records on all the traditional fronts: it carried more people than any other steamer afloat; it crossed the Atlantic faster; its comforts were augmented by a

Deck scene in the 1880s.

German band which played *Nearer my God to Thee* on Sunday mornings. Whether passengers found this a dubious choice of hymn is not recorded.

By now well-practised in the competition business, Cunard replied to the challenge with the 'pretty sisters' *Caronia* and *Carmania*, with the turbine-powered *Lusitania* — later to become a synonym for the horrors of war — and with the outstanding *Mauretania*, also turbine-powered, which held the record as the fastest ship on the Atlantic run from 1909 until the 1930s. The *Mauretania* had inbred elegance and speed as a matter of course; much rarer, she had 'soul'. People loved her just as, later, they would love the *Queen Mary*.

Predictably, the White Star Line — now part of the steamship combine owned by the American millionaire J. Pierpont Morgan — hit back by planning two ships that were even bigger, even faster, even more beautiful still. They were the *Olympic* and her sister the *Titanic*.

The pair started off with every advantage that their owners could give them. The *Olympic* — yet another 'biggest ship in the world' — had triple screws, a Louis XVI dining-room, Turkish baths with decor to match and — a total novelty — a swimming-pool. The *Titanic* was

The *Connector*, an inspired but unsuccessful attempt in the 1860s to produce a ship that would stand up against rough seas.

just as elegant and even bigger. Both, as a matter of course, carried radio; it had, after all, been the radio officer on the White Star's *Republic* who had become a world hero the year before by continuing to put out the CQD — 'Come quickly, danger' — signal as his ship slowly foundered under him. (He stayed by his transmitter for a solid fourteen hours; thanks to his efforts, all but a few of the *Republic*'s complement were saved.)

In addition, the *Titanic* had somehow collected the ultimate in temptations to providence: the floating palace to end them all was firmly and literally believed to be unsinkable.

The 'unsinkable' ship set out on her maiden voyage from Southampton to New York on 10 April 1912. After the stop at Queenstown the next day, her complement was 1316 passengers and 891 crew. However, and this was one of the factors that proved so decisively fatal, she had lifeboat space for no more than 1178—some 53 per cent of the places needed. Just before midnight on 14 April, in clear, calm, freezing weather,

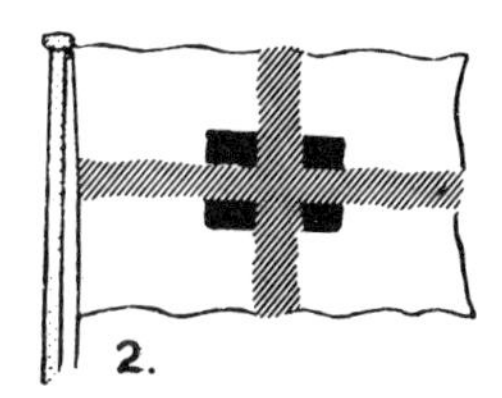

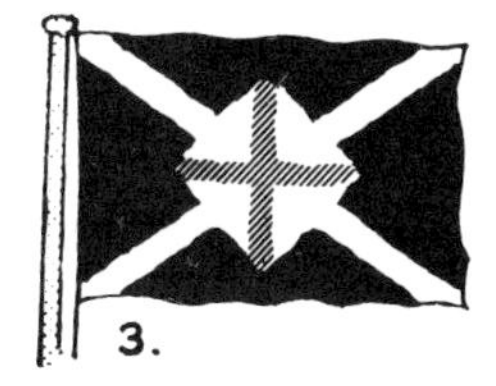

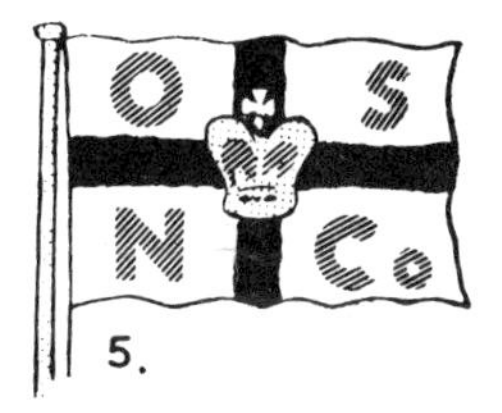

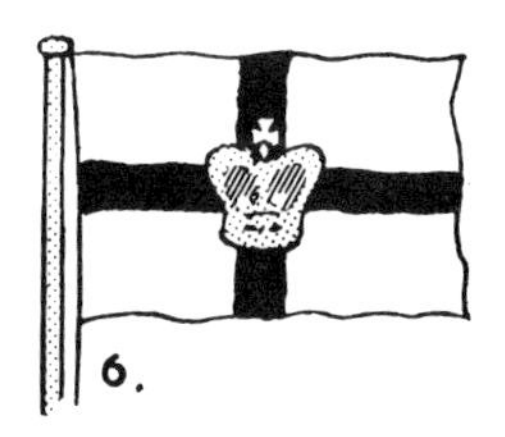

Evolution of a house flag. From top to bottom the flag as displayed on: Orient Line clippers, 1877; ships of F. Green & Co, 1878; the combined Orient S.N. Co, 1878, 1880, c 1892 to 1908.

lookout Frederick Fleet spotted something blacker than the night dead in front of him (there was no moon) and reported: 'iceberg right ahead'. The liner instantly altered course, but not quickly enough. The iceberg, casually grazing along the ship's hull, gashed a hole three hundred feet long. Her 'unsinkable' reputation was based on the fact that she could float with any two of her sixteen watertight compartments flooded; the iceberg had torn a hole in five of them. Two and a half hours after the initial collision, the great *Titanic* gradually tilted forward, reached the perpendicular and started her slide down an invisible two-mile slope to the bottom of the Atlantic. As described by Walter Lord, whose *Night to Remember* cannot be matched either as an example of meticulous research or as compulsive and terrifying reading, the passengers who had made it into lifeboats:

> could hardly believe their eyes. For over two hours they had watched, hoping against hope, as the *Titanic* sank lower and lower. When the water reached her red and green running lights, they knew the end was near . . . but nobody dreamed it would be like this — the unearthly din, the black hull hanging at ninety degrees, the Christmas card backdrop of brilliant stars . . . When the sea closed over the flagstaff on her stern, she was moving fast enough to cause a slight gulp.

The loss of the *Titanic* devastated the world. It was unbelievable — and yet it had happened. The total death-toll of that night was 1502. Of the first-class women and children passengers, 97 per cent survived, along with 32 per cent of the men, as against only 42 and 16 per cent respectively of the women and children and men travelling third-class. White Star was, in fact, cleared of the subsequent charge that third-class passengers had been unfairly treated, but no one actually disproved the allegation that they had not been allowed out of their allotted shipboard area quickly enough.

From today's standpoint, this was probably the most tragic element of the whole tragedy. The *Titanic*'s contemporaries focused their outrage on a slightly different target. The grief and horror that greeted the news of the 1502 deaths was mixed, covertly at first and then less covertly, with the feeling that God was not mocked. Why was the ship so plush? In the *Titanic*, the shipping world had lost track of what it was meant to be about: providing safe conduct through danger. The food, the gilded mirrors, the fun and the speed were all of minor importance compared with this. Nothing could disguise the fact that, in an area known to be studded with icebergs, the *Titanic* had steamed into one at twenty-two knots.

'You were sacrificed to the greedy Goddess of Luxury and her consort the Demon of Speed, is how one commentator addressed the 1500 dead. Tastelessly florid though his words sound now, he was right.

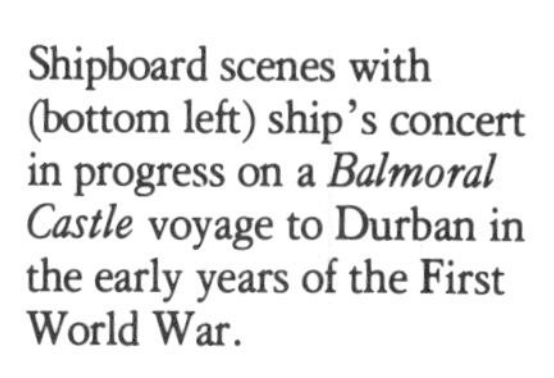

Shipboard scenes with (bottom left) ship's concert in progress on a *Balmoral Castle* voyage to Durban in the early years of the First World War.

7. *Stars of the Lines*

It would be an over-statement to say that, after the *Titanic*, things were never the same again. Shattering though the lesson had been, it would take time for its more subtle implications to sink in. The floating palaces, with their marble washstands, swimming-pools, barrels of *foie gras* and rigid divisions between the luxury and below-stairs trade, continued almost as if nothing had happened, although the safety angle, to be sure, suddenly loomed as important in the general sea-going consciousness as it had always done in Cunard's.

The *Titanic*'s successor — her intended name, *Gigantic*, was hastily replaced by the less fate-provoking *Britannic* — had an improved system of watertight bulkheads, and her complement of lifeboats was prominently displayed. The monster German newcomer, the *Imperator*, turned out to be literally unbalanced by her load of grandeur; to correct her awesome rolling, the funnels were shortened, her bottom lined with 2000 tons of concrete, and loads of mahogany and marble stripped away. But the basic tradition of the sea-going hotel remained unchanged and, as in hotels and restaurants today, expressed itself in thematic terms that grew ever more fanciful. On the *France*, super-rich passengers could enjoy a voyage in royal style, with their own Empire dining-room and a *salon* imitating that of a French *château*. The *Imperator* had a swimming-pool inspired — at considerable remove — by a Greek temple. And a third brand-new floating palace, the Cunarder *Aquitania*, played the *motif* game to the utter limit. There were Tudor rooms and George III rooms; there were memories of Inigo Jones, Christopher Wren and Versailles. There was a Pompeiian swimming-bath and an Olde English garden lounge. Modern steak-houses, with their Hawaiian bars, Sherlock Holmes grills and richly-written menus full of sun-kissed corn, have nothing on the *Aquitania*: 'You may', one description ran, 'sleep in a bed depicting one ruler's fancy, breakfast under another dynasty altogether, lunch under a different flag and furniture scheme . . . have your afternoon cup of tea in a verandah which is essentially modern and cosmopolitan, and

The horror of the *Titanic* lives on: film poster from 1953.

return to one of the historical periods experienced earlier in the day for your dinner.'

The same observer pointed out that, whether passengers dined under the auspices of Imperial Rome or Old Dixie, they would invariably appear in 'very modern evening dress'. William Cobbett's injunction to 'prepare suitable, but very cheap dresses for yourself, wife and children, to wear on board the ship' belonged to another world, and even Cunard's reminder to *Campania* passengers that 'it is not usual to dress in the evening for dinner . . . dresses of serge will be found very suitable' was distinctly out of date. Transatlantic voyages were now stylish affairs, serviced by valets and personal maids, and called for four or five changes of clothes a day. Jewellery, of course, was extremely important; of all the items in her baggage, the jewel-case was the only one that a lady would habitually carry herself. Once on ship, she would deposit this with the purser and join the pre-dinner queue each evening to withdraw the earrings and necklace of her choice. As the *Titanic* entered her death-throes, several women tried to retrieve their property from its official guardian; possibly a selfish move, but an understandable one.

The time was very close, however, when the socialites in the *Aquitania*'s Palladian lounge would be replaced by a totally different clientele: soldiers, splinted and bandaged; nurses with wide white veils; military doctors in khaki. The ship was launched only a few months before the outbreak of the First World War. From this point, nothing, on sea or land, would ever be the same again. By 1918 the whole world would have changed, and sea travel with it.

The war shattered sailing schedules along with everything else. Some ships switched almost within days to war work; others, having ended up in the wrong place at the wrong time, were interned for the duration. On the India run, half of the newly-amalgamated P & O/British India fleet of 200 ships was put to work as armed cruisers, troopships and munitions transports within two months. A brand-new addition, the *Kaisar-i-Hind*, was soon to enjoy fame as the luckiest ship afloat; one U-boat torpedo missed her by a hundred feet, another by fifteen and another by inches. A fourth, just before the end of the war, scored a direct hit — but both the ship and the 3500 people on her lived to tell the tale. The torpedo slammed into her by the fore-stokehold and, by a freak of chance, failed to explode. Underwater, *Kaisar-i-Hind* was painted red, but for two decades after her miraculous escape the heroically dented plates that had suffered the impact were picked out in a bright contrasting green.

On the Atlantic, the great Cunarders and their rivals were similarly active. One of the first in the fray was the 'pretty sister' *Carmania*, now anything but decorative in her armour-plate and sandbags. In a tough but faintly ludicrous encounter, she pulled off the tremendous

The *Cap Trafalgar*.

coup of sinking the German *Cap Trafalgar* in the south-west Atlantic. What gave the affair its Tweedledum and Tweedledee effect was the fact that the *Cap Trafalgar* (owned by Hapag and plying the South Atlantic run) was also a former luxury liner, and a much more luxurious one than her opponent. Far more evenly matched for size than either had expected — both were on the search for smaller fry — the pair went at it hammer and tongs; the *Carmania*, riddled with holes and burning hard, was almost at her last gasp when the *Cap Trafalgar* 'fell over' sideways, heaved and went down. In the spirit of a world that was soon to be murdered in the Flanders' fields, the men of the *Carmania* let off a cheer for their honourable adversary.

Up in the Mediterranean, other floating palaces were working just as hard, though less dramatically, for the war effort. The elegant *France*, the *Mauretania* and the *Olympic* joined the *Aquitania* as personnel carriers and hospital ships. With their great speed and size, they seemed almost purpose-built for ferrying troops, whole or wounded. The latter were placed as high up in the ship as possible so as to be near the lifeboats. Restaurants, gymnasia, smoking-rooms and pillared lounges were crammed with iron bedsteads, while nurses and doctors lived in the pre-war splendour of the lower decks. The *Titanic*'s successor, the White Star's *Britannic*, also entered the troopship business, but less successfully than the other four. These survived; the *Olympic*, in fact, had come off best in an encounter with a U-boat by simply running over it. But the *Britannic* struck a mine on her sixth

The *Carmania*.

Artist's impression of the sinking of the *Lusitania*.

Mediterranean run and sank — bows first, like her tragic sister — within an hour. However, all but a few of those aboard were saved.

But *the* shipping disaster of the war was, of course, the loss of the *Lusitania*. In the wake of the London blitz, the bombing of Dresden, the dropping of the atomic bomb on Hiroshima and Nagasaki and the horrors of Vietnam, this example of the effects of total war has lost some of its impact, but at the time it was compared with the worst excesses of the Indian Mutiny. The Cawnpore Massacre, it was felt, had now been superseded as the definitive example of foul inhumanity by this deliberate drowning of 1198 innocent people.

Unlike the majority of her kind, the *Lusitania* had stuck to her peace-time trade of ferrying civilian passengers across the Atlantic. Her main concession to wartime conditions was to economise on fuel — but, even so, she was still fast enough to out-distance any enemy attackers. Furthermore, it was then an accepted convention of war that a ship carrying civilian passengers would not be sunk until those passengers had been taken off. The *Lusitania* was thus thought to be doubly protected, until, just after lunch on 7 May 1915, she steamed up to the Irish coast and into the view of U-boat commander Walther Schwieger. To begin with, Schwieger thought he had spotted a positive flotilla of ships; his first glimpse of the *Lusitania* was of 'a forest of masts and stacks'. As the 'forest' came nearer, he realised his mistake. He dived, waited and let off his next-to-last torpedo at a range of 400 yards. On board the liner, a passenger who had been admiring the Old Head of Kinsale watched, hypnotised, as a streak of white darted towards the ship; the next second, he was lying on the deck, surrounded by geysers of steam, dust, debris and water. Within half an hour the

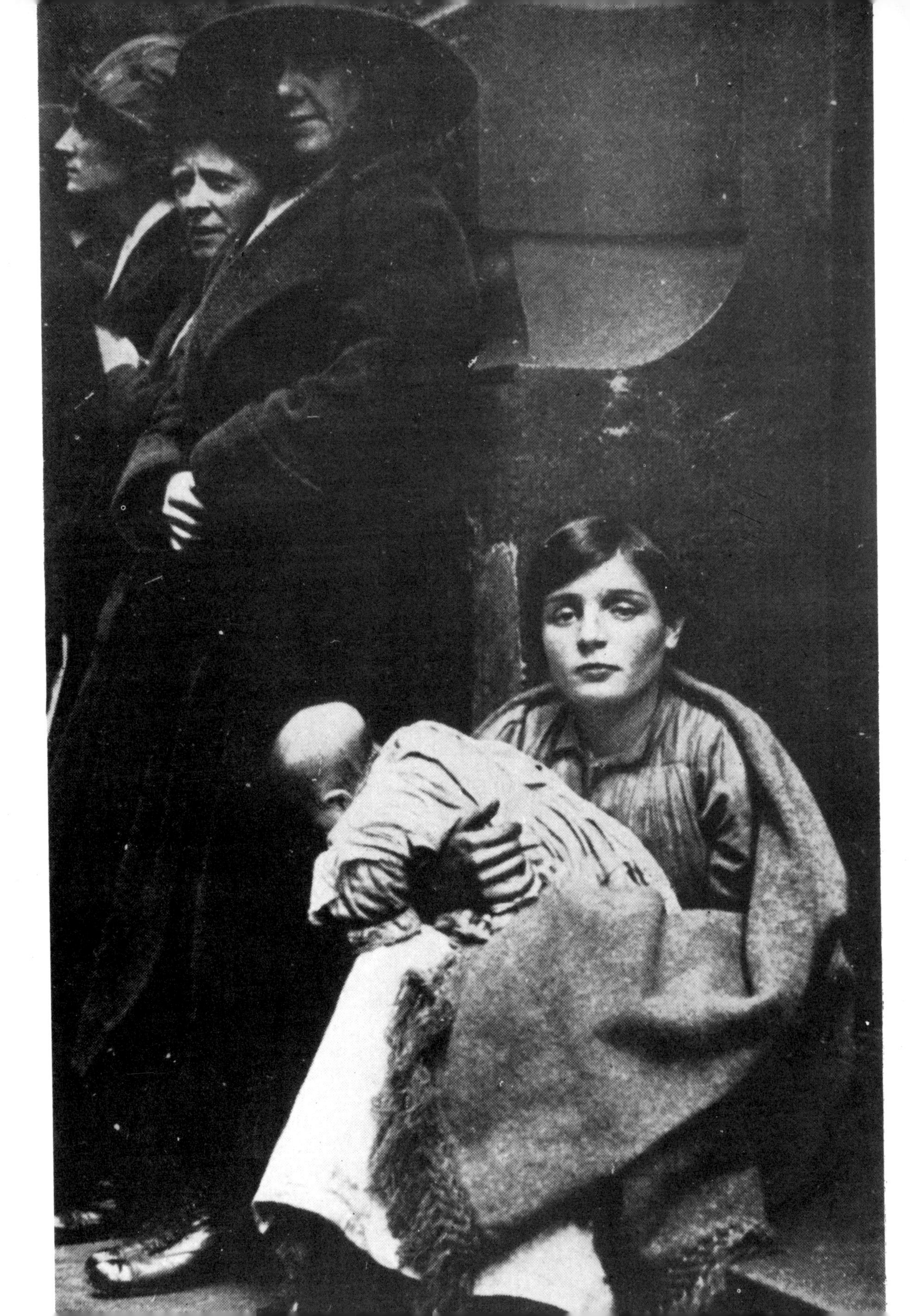

Captain Turner, master of the ill-fated *Lusitania*.

Opposite: relatives anxiously await news of the *Lusitania* in an all-night vigil.

Lusitania went down, carrying hundreds trapped inside her hull. The English-speaking world responded with a bellow of outrage; the fact that a newspaper warning to prospective passengers had been published by the Germans was brushed aside, and newspapers competed to find the most blood-chilling synonym for 'brutality'. The Germans protested that the *Lusitania* had in fact been sunk by the explosion of the ten tons of munitions in her cargo; the British, having none of this, retaliated with screams of 'murderers!' And the hitherto neutral Americans began to think twice about their neutrality. It would be — and has been — argued that Schwieger's next-to-last torpedo lost Germany the war.

When hostilities ended in 1918, it became apparent that other German losses were on the way. Her resources were briskly carved up among the victors, her warships and aircraft surrendered, and her trio of super-steamers — *Imperator*, *Vaterland* and *Bismarck* — shared out between Britain and the United States. White Star — now a British firm again — got the *Bismarck*, later to be renamed the *Majestic* and inspected by Queen Mary (she liked the kitchens); Cunard gathered in the top-heavy *Imperator*, which promptly proved herself a mixed blessing. One particularly uncomfortable voyage culminated in something more up the Pied Piper's street than a naval engineer's: the hordes of rats living deep in the ship were flooded out and sought drier quarters on the passenger decks above. The ship's idiosyncrasies got a further frantic going over, a new name — *Berengaria* — was painted on her sides and new colours on her funnels, and she joined the war veterans *Mauretania* and *Aquitania* to make up Cunard's Big Three of the 1920s. The owners, along with White Star and the rest, looked forward confidently to a rush of post-war business.

They nearly didn't get it. It was all very well for duchesses and plutocrats to honour liners with their presence, but the solid underpinning of the whole operation was still the handful of dollars a head paid by the steerage passenger. Just before the war the annual emigration rate from Europe to the United States had topped the million mark; shortly after it, the United States decided that enough was finally enough. From 1921 onwards, only 3 per cent (reckoned on 1903 figures) of a country's population were to be admitted. To make things worse from the shipping lines' point of view, the United States and its passenger ships had gone 'dry'. For all but teetotallers, ships like the American-owned *Leviathan* — formerly the German *Vaterland* — were dead ducks. Furthermore, on the other side of the world, potential travellers were beginning to take events such as Japanese earthquakes, Chinese civil war and Australian droughts into account; even the great P & O was having its nervous moments. Frissons were running round one shipping boardroom after another, when a solution suddenly emerged. In essence, it was nothing new; but it once and for

TO admit you've never been abroad is often as embarrassing as being unfamiliar with the classics. In the life of today one is as essential as the other. Of course, when you go, travel correctly. Choose either a White Star, Red Star or Atlantic Transport liner. It makes no difference whether you go First Class or TOURIST Third Cabin. You meet the world's charming cosmopolitans. The life on board, social and sports, is diversified, interesting and always thoroughly enjoyable. But if you are esthetic by nature the comfort of the salons and the out-of-way nooks on the broad decks have a strong appeal.

WHITE STAR LINE

RED STAR LINE · ATLANTIC TRANSPORT LINE

INTERNATIONAL MERCANTILE MARINE COMPANY

No. 1 BROADWAY, N. Y., OUR OFFICES ELSEWHERE OR AUTHORIZED AGENTS

all pointed the way that all super-scale sea travel was ultimately to take. The answer was to scrap the notion of steerage, replace it with 'tourist class', and pretty up the former steerage quarters to the point where young, cost-conscious, culture-hungry, fun-loving or plain old-fashioned thirsty Americans would not balk at a below-stairs passage. (Following the Three Per Cent Act, the transatlantic trade had become predominantly a New World affair.) It was no simple task to erase folk-memories of the old steerage days; but it was done. 'Such a jolly idea,' said one company, pushing hard; 'coziness and friendliness more than compensate for any lack of the sumptuous.'

Cosy it certainly was; one 'tourist third cabin', photographed in the mid-twenties, looks not unlike a rail sleeping compartment today, only with four bunks. Still, there were nicely-laundered towels, a proper washbasin, and even a fern in a pot to brighten it all up — and its potential inhabitants took to the 'jolly idea' with enthusiasm. Pushed into it by the emigration bar, and considerably helped by Prohibition, the refurbished, reorganised and now oil-fired liners could from this point on start going all out for the leisure market.

Their success was immediate, but the new shipboard regime was not welcomed by all passengers. One lady said it all when she complained that the real rest of a sea voyage had gone forever. 'No one', she added crossly, 'can take the shortest nap, there is such universal "doing something" noise.' The row would probably have been at its worst on the *Mauretania*, which made a point of drawing custom from the richest and brightest of American Bright Young Things. 'Her clientele', said a publicity writer, 'are very gay, always, very chic; her sailings are gala nights, with the Junior League at its most junior visible all over the lot . . . . You will find her decks populous with young girls and young men who more nearly than any other flesh and blood young girls and young men look like the drawings in *Vanity Fair* and *Vogue*.' The *Berengaria*, by contrast, aimed at out-and-out Top People — 'her passenger lists are electric with great names' — while the *Aquitania* was blue-blooded, refined, *très snob*. But even on the *Aquitania*, the Cunard man went on, indolent conversation alternated with 'energetic sport', and in a wider sense both energy and sport started the minute the sea-farer climbed aboard. There were friends to greet, enemies to cut or upstage, prospective husbands to mark down; Mamas ambitious for their Maybelles or Daphnes found a sea voyage as productive as several coming-out balls. There were the professional gamblers to spot and avoid; keen amateurs to find and fraternise with. There were the arrangements for drinks to locate; on French ships, personnel were given a crash course in English that put great stress on bar-keeper vocabulary. For the *crème de la crème*, there was the burning question of whether they would be invited to sit at the captain's table; for everyone, there was the even more important business of reserving a

Oppostie: 1929 advertisement for the White Star Line.

Visit Europe now and sail on American ships

BOOKINGS for the coming season indicate the great popularity of United States Liners. The travel-wise have taken the hint: they're going over in April and May, when there's more room on board; a wider choice of accommodations; European hotels and resorts are at their best; money's saved because of lower rates. Those who *must* vacation in summer are booking passage *now,* since they know why these ships are so much in demand: courteous, attentive stewards who speak your own language; a famous cuisine; cozy, home-like, luxurious staterooms; high American standards of comfort throughout the ships.

Your friends will know that you are travel-wise if you plan your trip at once on the speedy *Leviathan,* the world's largest liner, or on one of the five delightful cabin ships, *George Washington, America, Republic, President Harding,* or *President Roosevelt.*

United States Lines

FORTY-FIVE BROADWAY, NEW YORK CITY

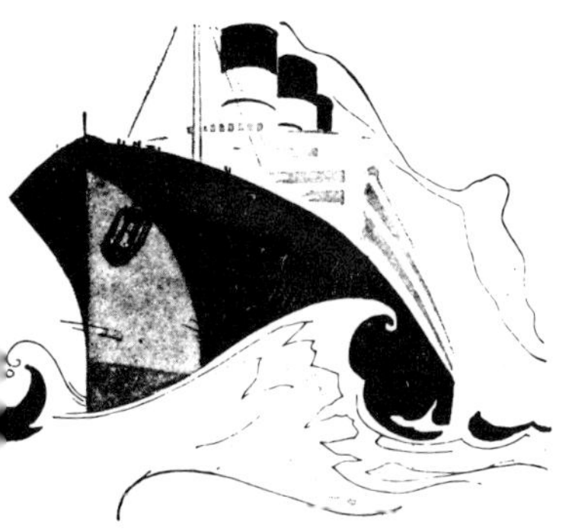

Above and opposite: two advertisements tempting Americans Europe-ward, in the 1920s.

well-placed deck-chair. On the transatlantic run, POSH applied only to a round trip that started from England; since on this route the sun was something to seek rather than avoid, Americans sailing eastward fought for deck chair positions that were SOPH.

If the cabin was your permanent base, your deck-chair was your daytime vantage-point. It was here that, cossetted, well-rugged and sustained by coffee, tea or soup (clear soup was a favourite mid-morning tipple), you observed clothes, manners, flirtations, mysteries and illnesses. Sea-sickness, of course, was still a force to be reckoned with; but for a good sailor there were few things more callously cheering than the sight of a limp fellow-passenger turning the colour of mistletoe. You also planned your strategies and wardrobe for the evening. Women in particular had to walk a tightrope between appearing over-casual and over-showy; ball gowns were in the worst of taste, but 'semi-dinner dresses' were all right. Fancy-dress parties, of course, were a different matter, since the aim was then to be as showily ingenious as possible; when a fancy-dress competition was in the offing, scarcely a corner of the ship went unraided for flags, sou'westers, glue, coloured paper, revolvers (the officers would loan these), nurses' uniforms, curtain-rings, canvas, tea-trays, cotton-wool and cork.

Fancy-dress, though, was tame stuff compared with the thrill of the auction pool. An important feature of shipboard life was betting in a sweepstake on the ship's daily progress, and in the first class cut-throat bidding would take place each night as tickets bearing a likely mileage total were auctioned. The correct answer, along with the ship's position, was announced every day from the bridge at noon and passed on to the anxious punters crowded into the smoking-room. One woman established a never-to-be-beaten record when she guessed lucky on the *Aquitania* for five nights in a row.

But not all shipboard entertainment was so highly organised. For every auction, concert, ball or cinema show that took place (frequently, in the case of film shows, in the lounge, home-movie style; ships' cinemas were a rarity), there would be a hundred or more small-scale, spontaneous do-it-yourself activities flourishing alongside. The simplest DIY game of all was walking. Five times round the promenade deck was usually a mile; hearty passengers stepped out with a will, perhaps hoping one day to equal the record set by an American doctor who clocked up a hundred miles in one Atlantic crossing (no one ever rivalled him). A more leisurely, but also more furtive, form of exercise was walking your dog. Pets could and did travel in style on the big liners but were usually confronted with large 'out of bounds' areas. However, some owners — notably Gertie Lawrence — often had a shot at unrestricted dog-walking, and their unfortunate pooches must have needed it. Travelling in luxury though they were, many of them showed all the symptoms of advanced constipation. They would not

The Palm Court on an inter-wars liner.

squat, they would not cock a leg; one or two liners tried to encourage them by installing sham fire-hydrants for their exclusive use.

But worrying about one's pet terrier was a highly specialised way of passing the time. More to the point, for the vast majority of passengers, was worrying about how to come first in one or more of the vast array of deck sports. There were extraordinary trials of mock strength, one of which was a cross between a Greasy Pole challenge and a pillow-fight; there were even more remarkable races. Beside the biscuit-and-whistle race (you took a mouthful of biscuit and tried to whistle a song through the crumbs), old favourites such as egg-and-spoon looked positively antediluvian. There were any number of variants on 'deck tennis', played with quoits. There were golf, billiards, a deckboard variety of lawn tennis; for obvious reasons, golf and tennis balls were fixed to a string. There was shuffleboard, once *shoveboard*, then *shovelboard*. And if all that failed to amuse, daring passengers had two more home-grown sports available to them. If they were third- or second-class, they could try infiltrating the glories of the first; and they could try to chat up the captain.

This could be an operation fraught with difficulty. As on the early steamships, and on the sailing-packets before them, a between-the-wars captain of a liner represented the pinnacle of shipboard society. In addition to bearing the ultimate responsibility for his ship and the thousands on her, he had to be a diplomat, a social charmer of formidable versatility, a Lord Spiritual (marriages at sea were relatively uncommon; burials were more frequent) and Temporal. Some took to this combination of roles with gusto, but others found themselves wilting under the strain and sought refuge in brusqueness or sly irony. One went as far as developing a whole speech wherewith to confound the chatty passenger.

> I have crossed the Atlantic 422 times; this will be my 423rd. I have not been shipwrecked or cast away on a desert island or been burnt at sea or marooned or shanghaied or caught by sharks and I don't want to be the ship is doing fifteen knots and could do more if she were going faster you will be able to go ashore as soon as we are alongside the jetty and not before and if you have anything you want to smuggle I don't want to know about it and I don't know the best way to get it ashore without paying duty I hope to retire from the sea some day *Is there anything else you would like to know?*

While passengers disported themselves, captains toiled at their multiple roles and stewards grew quietly wealthy (many of them, thanks to lavish tips, earned more in a year than their captains), the men back at head office decided that the time had come to get the drawing-boards out again. The new passenger markets seemed assured; what was needed was some new ships. That they would be fast, safe and luxurious went without saying, but the economic thinking behind them was something new. In the post-First World War era, the old problems of regularity and cost assumed a supreme importance. To be competitive, a line now had to offer a service regular as clockwork — and this service had to be maintained with as few ships as possible. On the Atlantic, two was the ideal, and suddenly everyone started thinking in terms of pairs. (P & O, working the East, tripled the formula and thought in terms of six.) Remarkably quickly, the results came grinding down off the slipways and, as they did so, gave a marine demonstration of the new forces at work in Europe. Germany, back in the running again, came up with the *Europa* and the *Bremen*, which recaptured the Blue Riband from the *Mauretania* by crossing the Atlantic in four days seventeen hours. Italy contributed the *Rex* and the *Conte di Savoia*; the idea had originally been to call the latter the *Dux*, but Il Duce, rather surprisingly, said no. From France came the super-modern *Île de France* and the superb *Normandie*, which in 1935 effortlessly broke all records with a maiden crossing of four days three hours. And Cunard, of course, held a pair of Queens.

To begin with, these had plainer names: Hulls 534 and 552. The former first took shape on the drawing-board in the 1920s and — like all her future rivals — was designed to take part in the 'largest and fastest' stakes. Cunard chairman Sir Percy Bates summed up the issues involved in a very few words.

> The speed is dictated by the time necessary to perform the journey at all seasons of the year, and in both directions, plus the consideration of the number of hours required in port on each side of the Atlantic.

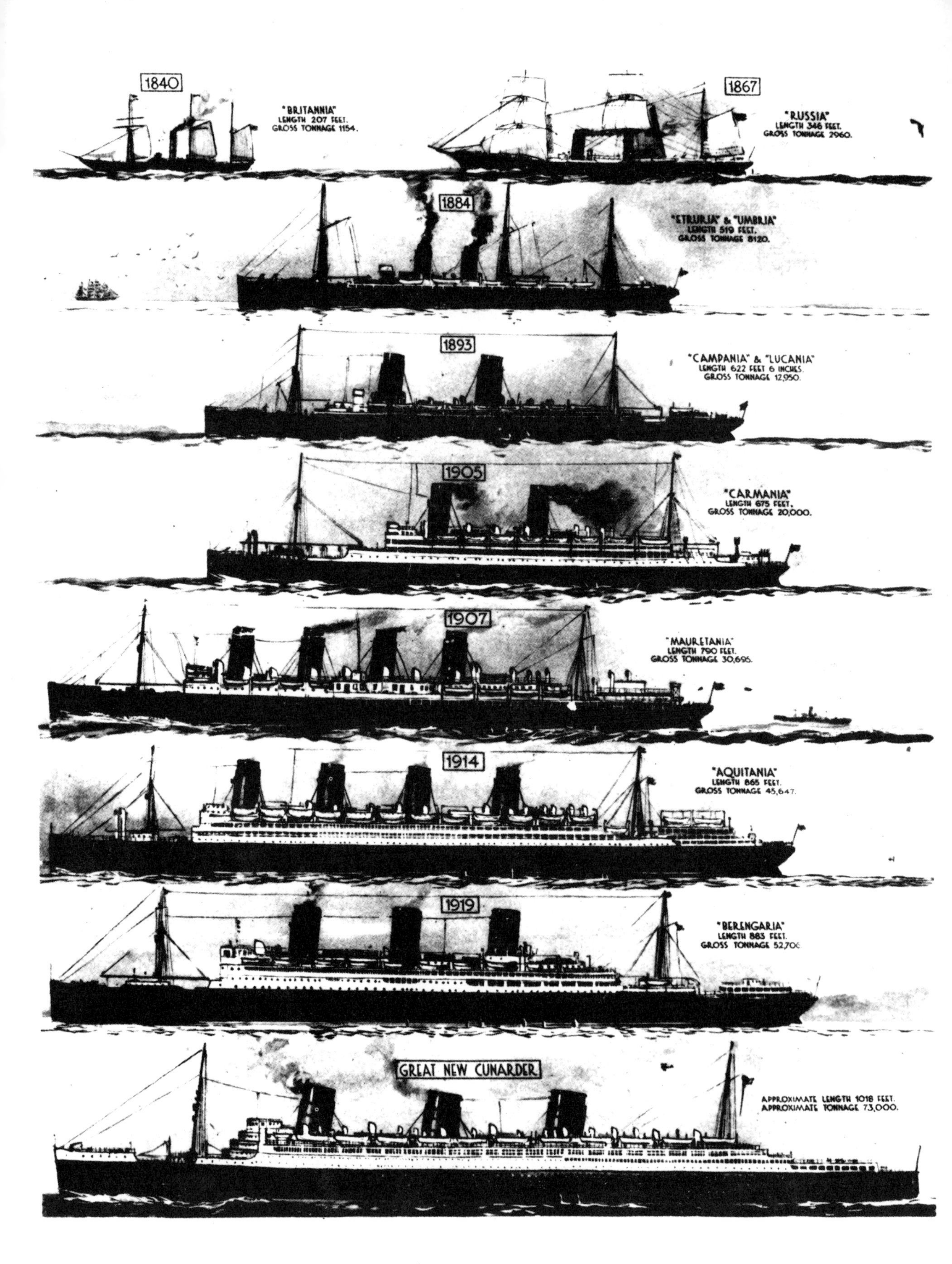
1840
"BRITANNIA"
LENGTH 207 FEET.
GROSS TONNAGE 1154.
1867
"RUSSIA"
LENGTH 346 FEET.
GROSS TONNAGE 2960.
1884
"ETRURIA" & "UMBRIA"
LENGTH 519 FEET.
GROSS TONNAGE 8120.
1893
"CAMPANIA" & "LUCANIA"
LENGTH 622 FEET 6 INCHES.
GROSS TONNAGE 12,950.
1905
"CARMANIA"
LENGTH 675 FEET.
GROSS TONNAGE 20,000.
1907
"MAURETANIA"
LENGTH 790 FEET.
GROSS TONNAGE 30,695.
1914
"AQUITANIA"
LENGTH 865 FEET.
GROSS TONNAGE 45,647.
1919
"BERENGARIA"
LENGTH 883 FEET.
GROSS TONNAGE 52,706
GREAT NEW CUNARDER
APPROXIMATE LENGTH 1018 FEET.
APPROXIMATE TONNAGE 73,000.

Shipboard entertainment on the *Queen Mary's* maiden voyage.

The size is dictated by the necessity to make money by providing sufficient saleable passenger accommodation to pay for the speed.

In the opinion of its technical advisers, so far from attempting to construct steamers simply to compete with others in speed and size, the Cunard company is projecting a pair of steamers which, though they will be very large and fast, are, in fact, the smallest and slowest which can fulfil properly all the essential economic conditions.

It was economic conditions, however, that nearly finished off the projected super-liner and her owners with her. The laying of the keel on Clydeside coincided with the onset of the Depression; by 1931 Cunard had spent £1½ millions on Hull 534 and needed another £4½ millions to turn her great steel skeleton into a practical proposition as a money-maker. It was money the company did not have, and 534's builders were laid off by the thousand. It was small consolation to the company — and none at all to the men in the dole queue — that Cunard's great rivals, White Star, were also in trouble; the third *Oceanic* of their line had got as far as the planning stage but no further.

Opposite: the *Queen Mary's* ancestors, traced by an artist of the *Illustrated London News*.

The *Queen Mary* enters New York harbour at the end of her maiden voyage.

However, White Star's difficulties turned out to be the saving of both companies. Neville Chamberlain, then Chancellor of the Exchequer, conceived the idea of using the 534 as 'a lever for bringing about a merger between the Cunard and White Star lines, thus establishing a strong British firm in the North Atlantic trade', and the pair were offered a cheap loan of £9½ millions provided they combined forces. Cunard White Star Ltd called the Hull 534 team back, and work went on.

Then there was the question of a name. According to legend — all ships tend to collect instant myths, and Hull 534 was no exception — Cunard decided to maintain its tradition of *-ia* suffixes by calling the new creation *Victoria*. A company director, due to shoot grouse with King George V, agreed to use the occasion to get His Majesty's consent to the use of the royal name and set about it with more tact than effectiveness. The King — so the story goes — was asked if he would allow the new vessel to be named after the most illustrious woman who had ever been Queen of England. The King replied delightedly that he would ask her when he got home.

In fact, the name *Queen Mary* had been decided on from the first, as a way out of the *-ic*/*-ia* dilemma that the merger of Cunard and White Star had brought about. The problem came not from a royal misunderstanding but from the fact that ships' names, like those of companies, must be unique during their lifetimes. A *Queen Mary* already existed, in the wildly contrasting shape of a Scottish coaster. In the end, her owners agreed to rename her *Queen Mary II*.

On 26 September 1934, Her Majesty christened her brand-new namesake with a bottle of Australian wine — champagne was felt to be overdoing the Gallic influence — and the thousand-foot-long symbol of national pride was launched on her career before the awed gaze of 250,000 well-wishers. The awe was inevitable; this was the latest of the long series of 'biggest ships in the world'. When completed, she weighed more than the whole Spanish Armada put together and was taller than the Statue of Liberty. Each of her three red-and-black funnels was big enough to hold three locomotives side by side (or, if you liked, the hull of the first-ever Cunarder *Britannia*). Her power was equal to that of seven million galley-slaves, pulling in unison. Her electricity was carried by 4000 miles of cable.

Those were the bare bones; the rest — the accommodation for 1285 crew and 2000-plus passengers, the strip-lighting, the rubber-plants, the miles of carpets and linoleum, the acres and acres of exotic veneers — was equally impressive. By and large, the paying public loved the result, but the *cognoscenti* shuddered. 'Mild but expensive vulgarity' was one of the kinder verdicts. 'Teddy Bear' was another, 'pure Leicester Square' a third. All the same, the *Queen Mary* captured the imagination in a way that only the *Mauretania* and the *Île de France* had done before — and that no ship would do again. Even today, people look back on her with loving veneration; 'a wonderful ship' they say; 'wonderful'. The magic of the *Queen Mary* may well have been not only because of her clean-lined design but also a result of the economic story involved in her construction. She, like Britain itself, had been saved from further years of depression by an upturn in the economy.

Cunard's first Queen made her maiden voyage in May 1936 and waltzed off (or lurched; she rolled so badly that crockery was smashed by the hundredweight) with the Blue Riband after a three-day, twenty-three hour crossing a few months later. Meanwhile, her running-mate 552 was gradually taking shape. Bigger even than the *Queen Mary*, more streamlined and proudly dubbed by her creators the 'ultimate ship', the *Queen Elizabeth* was launched by Queen Mary's daughter-in-law as the Munich crisis loomed. Before she sailed on her maiden voyage, the world was again at war.

Six luxury liners on the inter-wars Atlantic run in New York harbour.

A. *President Roosevelt*, United States Line, completed 1922.

B. *Roma*, Italian Line, completed 1926.

C. *Bremen* IV, North German Lloyd Line, completed 1929.

D. *Liberte*, French Line, completed 1930.

E. *Pilsudski*, Polish Ocean Line, completed 1936.

F. *Nieuw Amsterdam*, Holland-America Line, completed 1938.

8 *Battleship Grey*

The last quarter of 1939 saw frenzied movements among the world's merchant shipping. The *Athenia*, an Anchor-Donaldson steamer carrying refugees and home-going Americans, had been sunk off Ireland by a U-boat mere hours after Chamberlain's announcement that Britain was at war, and thereafter no ship belonging to the combatants felt disposed to linger on the high seas. All of them — cargo carriers, tramps, yachts, passenger steamers and super-liners — dashed for home or friendly ports. The *Queen Mary*, a short way off New York's Ambrose Light, shot into harbour and stayed there. The *Bremen*, berthed in New York, set off in the other direction. Travelling north at top speed, she avoided air search parties, rounded the North Cape and sought refuge in pro-Axis Russia. The by-now elderly *Aquitania* turned up in Southampton and then gamely announced that she would make the crossing back; memories of the *Lusitania*'s fate ensured that her passenger-list was not as long as it might have been.

As Hitler's grip on Europe tightened, both high-seas safety and the number of friendly harbours shrank drastically. Stragglers ran the triple risk of bombing, submarine and surface attacks. Among the ships caught a long way from home was the Norwegian motor ship *Tudor*, whose troubles coincidentally gave the Scandinavians one of the grandest tipples they had ever known. One particular brand of aquavit — northern Europe's answer to whisky — is traditionally matured by a there-and-back voyage to Australia, packed in casks in the holds of Wilhelmsen Line ships. The *Tudor* was a Wilhelmsen, and when she left Oslo in 1939 her hold was full of the precious stuff. The first part of the aquavit's journey went according to plan: the *Tudor* left Oslo, passed Cape Town, turned round in Melbourne and arrived at Port Said. At Port Said she stuck, and her cargo, which had by now earned its brand-name of Linie ('equator-crosser'), was stored. The legend on the bottle continues the story. Bombed in Port Said, the aquavit was taken to Suez and went from there on the motor ship *Troja* to Fremantle, arriving in December 1941. In February 1942 it was shipped by the motor ship *Tijuca* via Cape Town and Freetown to

The *Queen Elizabeth*, built for luxury, but used in anything but luxury by thousands of troops.

Bristol, where it arrived in May 1942. 'Double Linie' aquavit is probably the only benefit to have emerged out of the chaos that the world's merchant shipping was now to face. In the war's first nine months alone, 800,000 tons of shipping were written off. Some ships, like the Holland-America liner *Westerdam*, were sunk at their very moorings: the Nazis intended to fill the brand-new Dutch steamer with stones and to use her to block the Maas, but local resistance workers got there first. The *Westerdam* stayed underwater in her berth until Holland was liberated.

Ships that managed to stay afloat were grouped into necessarily slow convoys, which played havoc with their carrying capacities. Many were pressed into government service. The great super-liners were, of course, as obvious a choice for troopship work as they had been in the First World War. As the first Christmas of the war came and went, the *Normandie* and the *Queen Mary*, biggest and fastest of them all, were still safely tied up in New York, waiting for their chance; but where was the *Queen Mary*'s bigger and faster sister?

The answer was: still on Clydeside; and Clydeside was not a safe place for a national symbol to be. The *Queen Elizabeth* might be safe from submarine attack, but attack from the air was a different matter, as was ground-level sabotage. Besides, the fitting-out basin she occupied was now desperately needed for repair work to naval ships. The *Queen Elizabeth* had to go west after her sister — and quickly. Only twice in the year would tides be high enough to float her downriver, and the first of these was on 26 February 1940. Since the second would be a whole six months later — months during which anything might happen — the February date automatically became the deadline for her departure.

The decision triggered off security arrangements that, as far as passenger liners go, can never have been matched before or since.

Obviously, there could be no concealing the biggest thing afloat once she had set off; but *Queen Elizabeth*'s only protection against an enemy who spotted her was her tremendous speed, and even that might not be enough. The answer was to make the enemy look the other way. Her 400 crewmen were told that she would sail for Southampton; hotel rooms were reserved there for her technicians, crates of supplies were delivered, and the George V dry dock was booked for the alleged checks needed on her steering equipment. When startled harbour officials demanded a docking plan for their monstrous client, they got one: a beautiful and hastily-composed fake. At the same time, a discreet — and genuine — message went off to New York: please clear Pier 90, north side.

The fugitive herself was meanwhile being prepared for her exploit. She started by almost missing the crucial flood tide of 26 February: an appalling fifty minutes went by as the Clydeside tugs struggled against the incoming current. Failure would have meant disaster, since a temporarily much more important vessel, the battleship *Duke of York*, was due to take over the Queen's berth on the next tide — and the Duke, too, could only be floated in on the highest of high water. But the Queen finally made it and, still carrying the remains of her launching gear, moved cautiously downriver for final attention from engineers and painters. The world's 'ultimate ship' would make her maiden voyage coloured a drab and — it was hoped — inconspicuous grey.

The security clamp-down lasted until the last possible minute. Even the captain, Jack Townley, had no official knowledge of his destination until one hour before the ship was due to leave. In the early morning of 2 March, a Queen's Messenger came on board with a packet of sealed orders, not to be opened until the *Queen Elizabeth* was at sea. The crew were told that they would not, after all, be going to Southampton, and those who were unwilling to make the ocean trip were landed and 'quarantined' until the ship had sailed. An hour after the messenger had arrived, the super-liner raised anchor, moved through the anti-submarine boom and, with a send-off party of destroyers and aircraft in attendance, zig-zagged out to sea.

It turned out that the meticulously-laid false trail had been essential. On the day that the Queen was due to dock at Southampton, a skyful of German bombers was waiting in readiness over the Channel. But by that time their quarry was hundreds of miles away, hurtling along at thirty knots or more towards the safety of Ambrose Light. No escort could keep up with her, so she travelled alone and in total radio silence. Loneliness, too, was the predominant feeling among the tiny handful of official passengers. Thanks to the frequent changes of course demanded by safety requirements, the trip took five days, and the company officials and technical staff who had come along to monitor

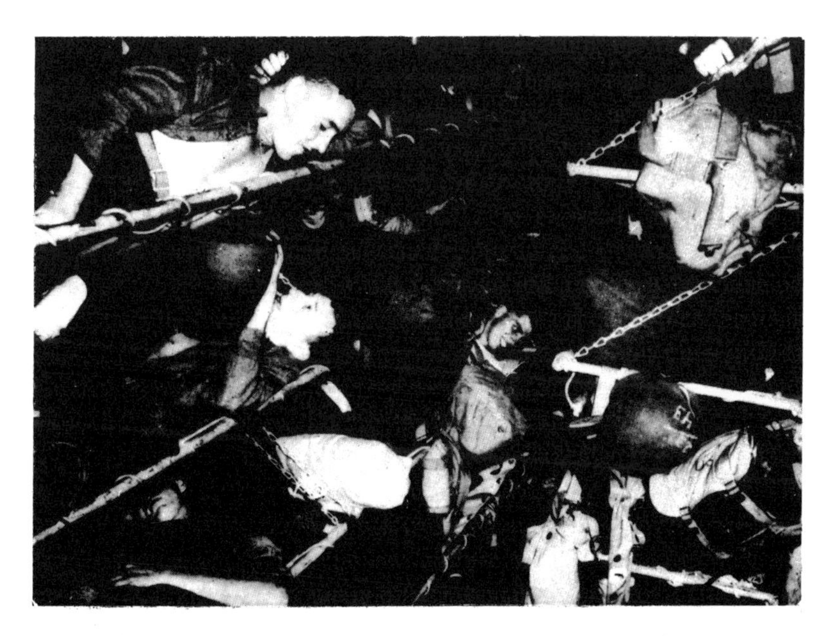

The new steerage passengers: troops on board the wartime *Queen Mary*.

the ship's performance spent the time in eerie luxury. They ate in a dining-room designed to seat 800 and took their pick among the cabins that were intended to accommodate 2000. The ghosts of future passengers must have been present in force; to chase them away, their real-life predecessors took to amateur dramatics.

While the Queen's departure had been shrouded in secrecy, her arrival in New York was not. The first sighting on the other side of the Atlantic was a significant one: it was from the air. Between the wars, regular air travel had started and, despite the diehards — 'I cannot believe that the airway will ever replace the seaway' said one Doubting Thomas — long-distance flights were now a practicality. It was a Transworld airliner that spotted a huge, seemingly deserted and badly rusting ship (the grey paint had not stood the crossing well) going for all she was worth towards the outer reaches of New York Bay. The *Queen Elizabeth* finally berthed alongside her sister and got a reception equal to that given to the paddlers *Sirius* and *Great Western* just over a hundred years before.

Her respite was short. Within six months, she was off to Cape Town and Sydney. The *Queen Mary*, equipped with wooden bunks and hammocks for 5500 troops, was already on war service, along with the *Aquitania*, the 'Empresses' of the Canadian Pacific Railway Company, the Royal Mail steamer *Andes* (the biggest ship on the Britain-South America passage), and the great P & O liners. A notable absentee was the pride of France's Compagnie Générale Transatlantique, the *Normandie*; she was still in her berth at New York where, late in 1941, she would be taken over by the United States and converted for Navy use. During conversion, sparks from an oxyacetylene torch fell on a bale of lifejackets stuffed with kapok, and the resulting tornado of fire, which took forty-three appliances to extinguish, brought her career to an abrupt end. Gutted and flooded, she rolled on to her side, sank down on the harbour floor and stayed there for eighteen months. Finally salvaged, she was never used again.

The other super-steamers, however, were used to the full, 'full' being the operative word. The liners built for the tropics gave relatively comfortable accommodation to the thousands of Allied troops that packed into them, but those designed for the North Atlantic proved hideously uncomfortable. The Queens operated a run from Sydney to Suez; on one occasion in 1941, driven close to breaking-point by the heat, crew-members of the *Queen Elizabeth* bickered, fought and ended by all but roasting a cook in his own oven.

The next year the *Queen Mary* also collected a black mark against her name. On 2 October, having returned to the Atlantic with her sister, she was carrying a routine load of 10,000 GIs to Britain when she collided with her escort cruiser, HMS *Curaçao*, and sliced her in half. Forbidden under any circumstances to turn round and thus risk an

The *Queen Mary* in dry dock for repairs to her bows after her collision with HMS *Curacao*.

The New World returns to redress the balance of the Old: GIs on board the *Queen Mary*.

enemy torpedo, the Queen ploughed on towards the Clyde estuary; both halves of the *Curaçao* sank and 338 of the 439 men aboard her died. Just why the two collided has never been completely explained and probably never will be. In essence, it seemed to be a matter of each of them making a wrong estimate of the other's next likely action. The Queen and her escort, which had joined her only that morning, were following the zig-zag tactics adopted by the *Queen Elizabeth* on her maiden voyage; those on the liner thought that the cruiser would keep out of her way, and for some reason the *Curaçao* did not keep out of way enough. A protracted legal action that followed ended with a House of Lords' confirmation of an appeal judgment that both ships had been at fault, the cruiser two-thirds to blame and the liner one-third.

The passenger load on board the *Queen Mary* at the time of the *Curaçao* tragedy was nothing out of the ordinary. She could, in fact, treble the capacity she had displayed on the Sydney-Suez run, and soon did. There was a war on; suddenly, the dreadful lesson of the *Titanic* had to be disregarded, and transatlantic travel speedily assumed some of the horrors of the old emigrant trade. Winston Churchill later explained how it happened: 'General Marshall asked me how many men we ought to put on board, observing that boats, rafts and other means of flotation could only be provided for about 8,000. If this were disregarded they (the two Queens) could carry about 16,000. I gave the following answer. "I can only tell you what *we* should do. You must judge for yourselves the risks you will run." ' And the Americans, to whom the Queens had been loaned for the duration, decided in the end that the risks were necessary. GIs were packed, piled and squashed into all available corners for their five-day dash to the aid of the Old World. During summer, many slept on deck (it was this that allowed the Queens' capacities to reach 15,000) and, at all times, a Box-and-Cox system operated for eating and bunking. Two men to a bunk was the rule; one soldier slept while the other watched films, gambled, received instruction about the British ('You sound just as funny to them but they will be too polite to show it') and joined interminable queues for 'chow'. This, while better than the food war-starved Britain could afford, was still ludicrously different from the glorious meals the liners had served in happier days. One GI understandably quailed when faced with *yesterday's* fried eggs, while thousands were dismayed by the prunes, cabbage and mutton that formed a staple part of the menu. Thousands more, however, were too far gone with seasickness to eat a thing. They collapsed in heaps along the railings, in the lavatories, on their bunks. The lavatories were always crowded, but every soldier had a wartime substitute for a chamber-pot — the deep-crowned helmet that, on arrival in Britain, would give the dumbfounded natives the idea that he was a Nazi. Someone still on his feet would wash it out afterwards. Five days is not long enough for a real seasickness martyr to find his sea-stomach, and plenty of GIs were incapacitated right up to the moment when they staggered ashore, but some were long enough at sea not only to recover but to gain a roaring appetite. Ocean memories collected by Norman Longmate for his study of the GIs in Britain include the following dismal account: 'We ate twice a day, 6 a.m. and 6 p.m. Starvation was assured because of seasickness in the mess hall four decks below — bad air, lousy food. However, by the third week — our trip took twenty-eight days in a slow convoy — we'd eat anything floating around.'

Bad food, the stench of vomit, sketchy opportunities for use of the lavatory and a twenty-eight-day crossing: the GIs could have been sailing-packet emigrants. One chilling fragment of old-time sailors' slang also found itself revived: instead of the 'coffin brigs', there was now 'coffin corner', the lead front corner position in a large convoy. But two elements of a GI crossing were totally new: wads of discarded chewing-gum covered the decks, and lovingly-carved graffiti adorned every inch of mahogany. The chewing-gum would be scoured off during a lightning-fast turn-round in Britain, but Kilroy stubbornly went on proclaiming his presence until the end of the war.

In 1945, village after British village woke up to find its resident Yanks, as much part of the scene as ration cards, had upped and gone. The ships they were travelling home in had made a contribution to the war that can scarcely be measured. Churchill himself ventured the estimate that the Queens alone had shortened the war by a year.

American servicement pack the *Queen Mary* as they return home after the war.

In 1946, the *Queen Mary* was inspanned to act as a maritime 'Orange Blossom Special' for over 12,000 GI brides and their babies, all journeying towards a new life in a country they had never seen. 'No baths,' one girl told Mr Longmate, 'and the showers are locked. I can see I shall arrive in New York looking like a tramp.' But the food, after the rigours of carrot pie and dried eggs, was dreamlike; cuisine worthy of the name had returned to the western ocean. For those who could eat it, the ice-cream and butter and candy were a typically transatlantic sign that things were now going to be all right.

To the world's shipping lines, the signs all seemed to point in the same direction. Their losses, in terms of both ships and men, had been terrible; indeed, twice as many merchant seamen died in the Second World War as had done in the First. But some of the grandest ships ever built were still safe, and it would not be long before the business of providing ocean passages reached new heights of glory.

That was the hope; the reality turned out to be different.

9 *'It Is With Great Regret . . . '*

In 1974, a friend of the writer got engaged. The marriage, it was planned, would take place early in the new year and, since the couple were due to move to Canada immediately afterwards, the idea of a brief but elegant honeymoon on board a transatlantic liner struck them as logical. They counted their cash, visited shipping offices — and found, to their extreme surprise, that the project was not on. Between Boxing Day and the beginning of March, not a single liner would that year make the centuries-old crossing between Britain and the New World. Undaunted, the pair changed their plans and got married in time to catch the Boxing Day sailing.

Even in Dickens' day, 130 years before, such a shift would not have been necessary: Dickens, after all, had put to sea on 3 January, in a boat very much smaller, more comfortless and less seaworthy than the one to which the honeymooning couple proposed to take their custom. By the turn of the century, they could have taken their pick of a dozen great shipping lines, all of them promising the utmost variety in entertainment, food, atmosphere and departure dates. In 1948, in a world still struggling to right itself after the Second World War, the North Atlantic run was maintained by no less than fifty-nine ships — a total that included the Cunarder *Queens*, at last operating the two-weekly shuttle service for which they had been built. Three years later, America would leap back into the battle for the Blue Riband by launching a liner that matched a destroyer for speed and a greyhound for elegance; on its maiden voyage, the *United States* succeeded in winning the prized trophy with a crossing a whole ten hours shorter than the best the *Queen Mary* had ever been able to do.

And yet, twenty-three years later still, two members of the travelling public that all these vessels had been expressly designed to serve found themselves unable to get what they wanted. Just what, in that tiny space of time, had gone wrong?

Up to a point, the answer is simple. Just as the steamers had displaced the sailing packets, so had the airliner displaced the steamers. Why spend days on the Atlantic when you could reach your destination

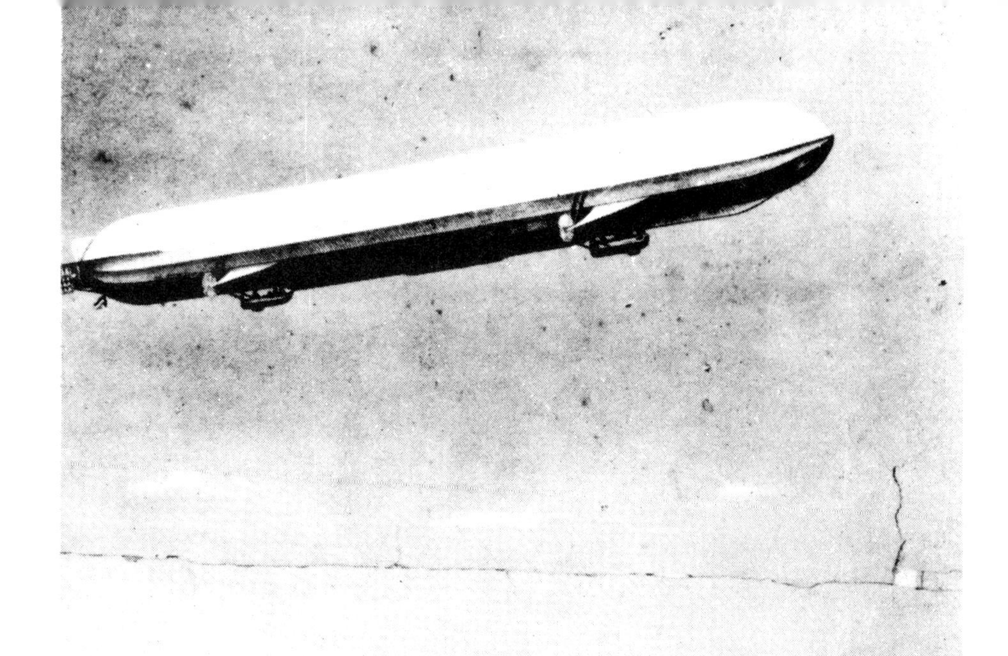

1930s poster for a German airship service: connections with the Hamburg-America Line's ships were possible.

within hours? But there was more to it than that. The starting-point for all technological progress — whether in steel furnaces, dentists' drills, or transport — is demand, steady and sustained enough to make technological innovation worthwhile. The innovation, if successful, then in turn creates further demand. In the case of air travel, the main impetus for one breakthrough after another came from the demands of war, and, when hostilities were over, those breakthroughs cried out for peace-time exploitation. The wood-and-canvas bomber of the First World War was the prototype of the 1920s airliner; the first jet — a fighter plane, the Gloster E28 — was rushed into existence in 1941, to the stupefaction of observers ('My God, chaps,' said one, 'I must

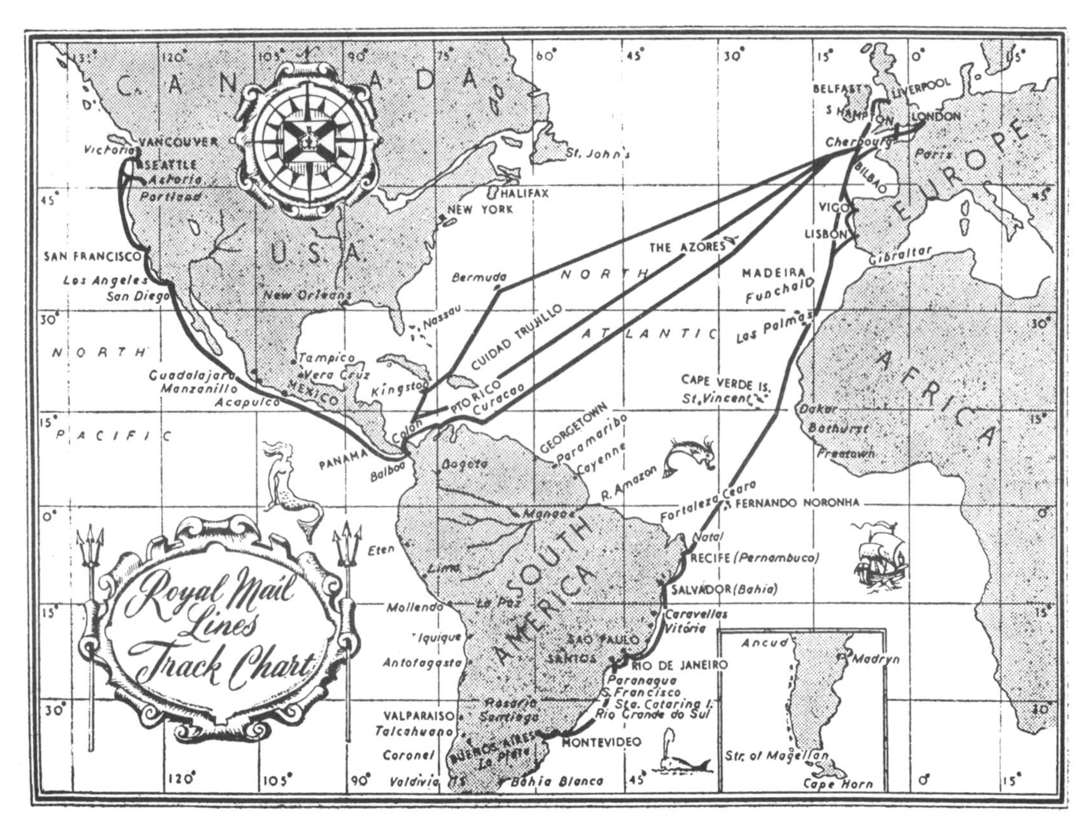

Track chart of the Royal Mail Lines showing its services in the early 1950s.

Opposite: 1952 advertisement for the United States Lines.

be going round the bend — it hadn't even got a propeller'). It was a foregone conclusion that, as soon as the war ended, aircraft manufacturers should think of transferring their latest wonder to civilian aircraft.

But, once transferred, would it catch on to the point where it became, not just commercially viable, but commercially triumphant? History is littered with examples of technological miracles that, against all expectation, didn't make the consumer grade. Given hindsight, Hero's 'steam engine' can be seen as an early one; more modern instances are the three-D film and the electric car, while in the world of shipping the *Great Eastern* casts its awe-inspiring shadow. And comparisons of aircraft passenger figures before and shortly after the war (210,400 in 1939 and 240,000 in 1948 on British airlines) did not appear to show a dramatic increase in interest in the idea of going by air.

By 1958, however, the total of those annually flying British had soared past the million mark. The jet airliner had succeeded, and brilliantly so, in creating a demand for itself. And it owed its success, not merely to its speed and the vastly improved passenger amenities that the airlines could now afford, but to something altogether more subtle. The Second World War, like the First, had brought sweeping

LONDON BOUND

REGULAR FAST SERVICES
PASSENGER AND FREIGHT
FROM UNITED KINGDOM & EIRE TO
NEW YORK BOSTON & U.S.A. PORTS

UNITED STATES LINES

Freight: 38 Leadenhall Street, E.C.3.
ROYal 6677.

Head Passenger and Executive Office: 50 Pall Mall, S.W.1.
WHItehall 5454.

Artist's sketch of a 1950s passenger cabin.

social changes in its wake, one of the most important of which was the enormous growth in buying-power among the wage-earning sectors of the population. From the end of the war onwards, the numbers of people who could afford to live well on unearned income — the people who before 1939 had formed the cream of the sea travel trade and also a substantial proportion of its bread-and-butter — would slowly but inexorably decline, while the numbers of those who lived well on their earnings would just as inexorably rise. Shipboard life was leisured, gentle, mannered and owed a lot of its charm to the way it represented a home from home to a nicely-graduated variety of social circles, the members of which had all the time and money they wanted for cultivating each other. It had little to offer a rising young executive of the post-war boom, who would have scorned those circles every bit as much as they would have scorned him.

In addition, the business truism 'time equals money' that had, in the early days, made the sailing packets race each other across the Atlantic was now introducing that same rising executive to the comfort and prestige of the businessman's air trip. It was natural that, as his salary increased and air travel grew relatively less expensive, he should buy air tickets for himself and his family when they went on holiday.

Meanwhile, the young and dashing among the hereditary rich had also begun to spurn cucumber sandwiches in the ship's lounge in favour of a glamorous leap into the skies — and, the status symbol of today being the supermarket purchase of tomorrow, the concepts of charter flights and package holidays were only a step away.

Happily for their peace of mind, none of this could readily be foreseen by the shipping companies as, at the end of the war, they took stock of their assets. Their war-time losses, though heavy, were certainly not such as to make them despair; Britain, still the leading shipping power in the world, desperately needed to start earning dollars again, and the general atmosphere was one of buoyant determination. The by now richly-diversified P & O Group, which had in all lost 182 ships, started to reconstruct its fleet: 'Much of this rebuilding', the Group comments, 'consisted of passenger liners: *Himalaya* and *Chusan* for P & O, *Orcades* and *Oronsay* for Orient Line, *Kenya* and *Uganda* for British India, *Rangitoto*, *Rangitane* and *Ruahine* for the New Zealand Shipping Company — *Iberia*, *Orsova*, *Arcadia* and, more recently, *Oriana* and *Canberra* followed.'

Union-Castle, which had lost seven of its great passenger vessels, promptly filled the gaps left by the two crack mail liners among them with two more, the *Pretoria Castle* and the *Edinburgh Castle*. The *Edinburgh*'s namesake, a mail steamer damaged not by enemy action but by sheer wear and tear as a depot ship in Freetown, was given a hero's funeral: too dilapidated to return to England, she was taken offshore and sunk by gunfire.

Canadian Pacific, the worst hit among the British shipping lines, at first found the cost of rebuilding from scratch too prohibitive, so the company neatly replaced its dead or dying 'Empresses' (one of which, the *Empress of Britain*, had been its flagship) by upgrading the two 'Duchesses', *Richmond* and *Bedford*, that it had left. The *Empress of Scotland*, formerly *Japan*, was still on the active list.

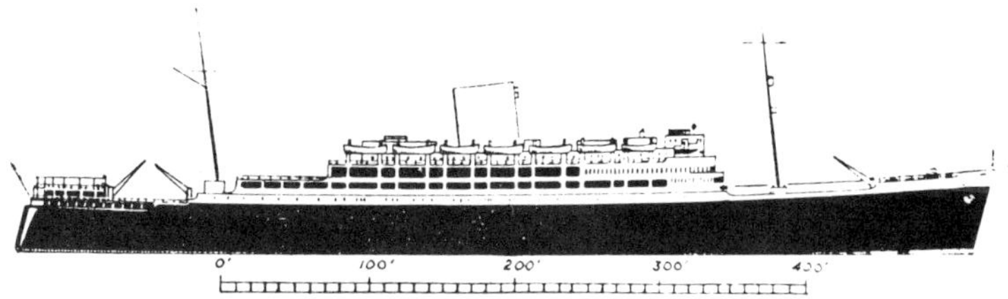

Profile of the *Andes*, launched in 1939.

This twice-named imperial consort was not, however, the only star liner to have come through the war in good working order. The much-loved *Île de France* was still functioning; so was the German *Europa*, now the property of France and re-christened the *Liberté*. Royal Mail still had its *Andes* which, like the *Queen Elizabeth*, had been launched too late ever to make a civilian maiden voyage. And, of course, the *Queen Elizabeth* herself and her sister were ready and waiting for normal life to resume. The painters came, and the carpenters, and the upholsterers: the battleship grey of war-time gave way to acres of smart black and shining white, while Kilroy's gouged-out messages were all removed. The *Mary* got a shipboard cinema, a wardroom for its engineers and some new murals; the *Elizabeth*, finally emptied for her standee berths for 10,000, her temporary lavatories and the storerooms that had housed those mountains of

Cocktail lounge on the *Queen Mary*.

mutton and prunes, was fitted out with all the appurtenances of civilised living that had been put in store during the war. With the help of New World sources of supply, the cuisine of the *Elizabeth*'s official maiden voyage in 1946 moved several stages further in the direction of the fabled transatlantic standards of between the wars: while grapefruit, shoulder of lamb and roast turkey may not sound very exciting today, they dazzled the maiden voyagers every bit as much as the American oranges and butter had delighted the GI brides on the *Queen Mary*. Understandably, several of the *Elizabeth*'s first paying passengers stuffed themselves to the point of digestive collapse. It would take some years' hard training before the ocean-going set could accept without even a murmur of gratified surprise the gallons of turtle soup, the hundredweights of chicken (broiling, squab, Guinea, roasting and *poussin*), the sturgeon, snails, nectarines and cream that would form the raw materials of later Cunarder cooking.

For the ocean-going set still, at that time, existed. Film stars and industrial tycoons, aristocracy and politicians and the international elite of sport all continued to use the *Queens* and their contemporaries. Aeroplanes might have the advantage of speed, but an ocean passage had style; to be able to afford the enforced leisure it demanded was stylish in itself. By now aware of the threat from the skies, the shipping lines built up the style angle for all they were worth, and their audience for a time responded. Passenger lists included Lord Beaverbrook, Winston Churchill, Rita Hayworth, Randolph Turpin, the Archbishop of Canterbury, and the Duke and Duchess of Windsor.

The Windsors were particular devotees of the extraordinary *United States*, which owed much of her warship-like efficiency to the fact that she had been designed to double as one. Smaller than the *Queens*, she could carry the same total of passengers or 14,000 troops; air-conditioned and superbly appointed, she was built with the huge fuel capacity and intricately-divided hull of a ship that might need to travel for days without stopping and to continue functioning even when partially damaged. She was also as fireproof as her designers could make her. Only her grand pianos and butchers' chopping blocks were of wood, while all the rest was a modern-as-tomorrow mixture of man-made fabrics, composition floors, steel and aluminium. The *United States*, in fact, was a ship first and a luxury human environment second. Thirty-nine years after the disastrous encounter between an iceberg and a ship that put the luxury side first, the travelling public had been presented with the *Titanic*'s final antithesis: ultra-comfortable, ultra-fast and ultra-safe, the *United States* can be seen as a culmination of a hundred-plus years' of steamship design and a keystone for all future development in the field of high-speed passenger shipping.

And she had come just too late. Before the 1950s were out, the number of transatlantic air passages had caught up with and passed its sea equivalent. After the crucial moment in 1958 when the two were neck-and-neck, there could be little doubt as to the outcome — air travel would continue to increase, sea travel to decrease. As far as straight competition went, the jets didn't have it all their own way: the rate at which steamer passages declined was less steeply-sloping than that of the increase in flight custom, so many of the airliners' passengers were new travellers altogether, as opposed to 'escapes' from shipboard life. But the ships were now continually missing their chances of adding this newly affluent section of the public to their clientele. The cabins and cocktail bars and sunlounges of the liners steadily emptied: the jets, with their packaged smoked salmon and Muzak, had won.

The *United States*: ultra-fast — but just too late.

Two liners of the Swedish-America Line, *Gripsholm* and *Kungsholm*, in New York harbour in the 1960s.

Faced with a shrinking market, ever-rising costs and millions of pounds' worth of capital tied up in unwanted chunks of steel, the shipping lines did the only thing they could. Following a trend that had first clearly defined itself between the wars, they took it to the ultimate: from now on, the leisure market would be the over-riding goal. The heyday of the cruise — of sailing comfortably from place to place, with no ultimate destination but the point where you'd originally started — had arrived.

As an idea, this form of holiday-making was anything but new. The honours for inventing it traditionally go to P & O, whose route through the Mediterranean and Egypt was positively studded with attractions for the cultured tourist. In an inspired stroke of public relations, the growing company gave William Thackeray a free ticket for a tour that took in Gibraltar, Malta, Constantinople, Jaffa and Alexandria, with time ashore for visiting Jerusalem, Cairo and the pyramids. 'So easy, so charming and I think profitable — it leaves such a store of pleasant recollections for after days' is how, in the book he subsequently wrote on the trip, Thackeray summed up his jaunt. As, through the nineteenth century, ships grew bigger and more comfortable, one shipping line after another had a shot at cruise-purveying; it was, after all, a simple way of filling up cabins during seasons when they tended to stay obstinately empty. The tradition of sun-seeking grew up and went on growing — and, by the end of the 1920s, the cruise had become firm favourite of the well-to-do. The lure continued to be that same ease and charm that Thackeray had promised and which, over a century after he promised it, still obtains: as this chapter was being prepared, an article in the *Observer* asked the question, 'Why put to sea to play ping-pong, go to fancy dress dances, lounge in a deck-chair or get drunk every day when all these diversions are just as available ashore?' The answer, writer John Sandilands concluded, was basically security: 'a daily routine that on the best type of cruise becomes akin to hospitalisation. Regular meals, a total absence of the horrors of choice of venue for food and diversion, of currency problems and taxis and foreign languages.'

To the shipping lines of the 1950s and 1960s, this hankering of the public for holidays without tears seemed to present the only way out of an extremely difficult situation. A period, in the right season, as a *bona fide* means of transport, with cruises during the rest of the year: that was to be the strategy of the future. As they grew obsolescent, the old luxury liners would go — most of them to the breaker's yard, the *Queen Mary* to her final berth as a Californian leisure centre, the *Queen Elizabeth* to her appointment with an unknown Hong Kong arsonist — and new ones, more fitted to their dual role, would take their place.

Cunard's description of its latest superstar is explicit as to her owners' intentions. The *QE2*, launched in 1967, was not, the company stressed, a modern version of the former Queens.

She is a resort hotel that has the advantage of being able to follow the sun, and includes in her itineraries many ports that her deep-draughted predecessors were

The first-class drawing room of the *Windsor Castle*.

incapable of entering . . . The ship that began to take shape on Cunard's drawing boards in Liverpool was actually the first large British ship planned and designed from the start to capture the cream of the North Atlantic trade in the season and the cream of the sun-seeking cruise market in the winter. The ship had to be dual-purpose, and flexible in the fullest sense . . . QE2 is not so much in competition with the air, which is transportation, as with land-based resort hotels, which are holiday and leisure centres.

The subject under discussion, with her service speed of 28½ knots, her four swimming pools and two libraries, her cinema, her print shop and laundrettes, hospital and dental surgery, bank and children's playground, is only one of the ships that today offer British seagoers a choice of two hundred cruises or more. Others in the cruise market include companies that hail from France, Norway, Greece and Finland. P & O, of course, is there, and so is Holland-America. But jagged gaps in the ranks are now appearing.

Royal Mail, for example, got out of passenger operations when the *Andes*, converted in the closing stages of her career into a one-class cruise liner, was withdrawn at the beginning of the 1970s. Royal Mail

Queen Elizabeth II, last of the great liners.

is part of the Furness Withy Group, to which Shaw Savill also belongs; the organisation as a whole ceased to operate passenger ships two years ago. Union-Castle/Safmarine, which at the beginning of 1977 was still offering both a transport service (with reduced fares for emigrants) and all-inclusive holidays, will stop doing so before the year is out. Said a starkly informative press release, dated November 1976:

> It is with great regret that Union-Castle/Safmarine announce that the two remaining passenger mailships operating on the route between the United Kingdom and South Africa are to be withdrawn from service in the latter part of 1977 . . . This is a direct result of the forthcoming introduction of a container shipping service on this route which will embrace the shipment of cargo presently carried by the mailships.

Indeed, readers of the daily press could scarcely escape the impression that the big ships were on their way out the world over. Two more to go were Italy's luxury liners *Michelangelo* and *Raffaello*, sold to the Persian Imperial Navy for £21 million. 'The *Raffaello*', the *Daily Telegraph* explained, 'will be anchored in the harbour of Bouchir and the *Michelangelo* at Bandar Abbas to be used as floating hotels for 1,500 people, among them officers and their families as well as 350 crew.'

Even P & O, which operates Britain's largest fleet of cruise liners and offers sailings from the UK, Australia and the west coast of North America, does so on a fleet of only seven ships. The Group's principal interests now tend to lie more with tankers, mini-submarines and — surprisingly — building.

As an elegiac advertisement for Union-Castle's last sailings pointed out, the causes of the continuing decline of passenger travel by sea are unavoidable. Rising costs and the switching of cargo to container ships

had, in this case, made the line's *Windsor Castle* and *SA Vaal* 'an unaffordable luxury to run'. The ocean-going liners depend for their functioning on what are now some of the world's most expensive commodities, notably service. 'And don't forget,' adds one shipping company spokesman resignedly, 'that potatoes cost us 15p a pound just as much as they do you.'

Put in simplest terms, the ships' income has not risen to meet expenditure. Just as big and beautiful private houses, hard to maintain single-handed and even harder to heat, are now being snapped up for prestigious office complexes, so are the big and beautiful ships going to permanent last homes as museums or floating quarters for armed forces. Their places in the world's docks are being taken by increasingly efficient cargo vessels, which do not need the stewards, waiters, bellboys, barbers, cooks and administrators that their more glamorous counterparts called for in such huge quantity. Cruising apart, sea travel is going back to what it was in its earliest period, an affair for the professionals only — and even cruising does not appear to offer the hope it once did. To observers, it looks like not the beginning, but the end of the end.

An ocean passage, in its day, has been a matter for dread, grief, admiration, envy and delight. And its day has been remarkably short. Inconceivable though its millions of participants would have thought it at the time, the phenomenon of organised mass sea travel has lasted a little less than two hundred years.

It is temping to wonder whether the jetliner — the apparently rock-hard foundation on which all long-distance travel is now built — will be as long-lived.

Opposite: ship-board life in the 1970s.

Acknowledgments

The publishers wish to express their gratitude to the following picture sources:
The Peninsular & Oriental Steam Navigation Company, pages 4, 7, 8, 9, 12, 14, 49, 53, 57, 58, 59, 60, 61, 64, 66, 67, 68, 69, 70, 71, 73, 74, 75, 76, 77, 79 and endpapers
Union Castle Mail Steamship Co Ltd, pages 119, 120, 122
Liverpool University, pages 19, 54, 55
Mary Evans Picture Library, pages 13, 15, 39, 41, 42, 43, 48, 50
Radio Times Hulton Picture Library, pages 10, 22, 52, 97, 98
Illustrated London News, pages 23, 30, 34, 38, 72, 88, 96
Broadwater Collection, pages 17, 36, 80, 90, 92, 93, 111, 113
Author's Collection, pages 64, 82, 83

Bibliography

American Notes, Charles Dickens, Baudry's European Library, Paris
Atlantic Conquest, Warren Tute, Cassell
The Big Ships. R. M. Wilson, Cassell
The Clipper Ship Era, A. H. Clarke, G. P. Putnam's Sons
The Cooking of Scandinavia, Dale Brown, Time-Life International
The Cunarders, Peter Barker Publishing Ltd, for the Cunard Line
Emigrants' Guide, William Cobbett, published by the author
Europe in the Fourteenth and Fifteenth Centuries, Denys Hay, Longman
Flight, Peter Lane, Batsford
Folk Song in England, A. L. Lloyd, Lawrence & Wishart
The G.I.s — The Americans in Britain 1942-1945, Norman Longmate, Hutchinson
A Hundred Year History of the OM P & O, Boyd Cable, Ivor Nicholson and Watson Ltd
Indian Cavalry Man, Freddie Guest, Jarrolds
Memoirs of a Bengal Civilian, John Beames, Chatto & Windus
A Night to Remember, Walter Lord; Longmans, Green
***The North Atlantic Run*, J. Maxton-Graham, Cassell**
Passage to America, Terry Coleman, Hutchinson
The Penguin Atlas of World History, Hermann Kinder and Werner Hilgemann, Penguin
Powered Ships — the Beginnings, Richard Armstrong, Benn
The Queens of the North Atlantic, Robert Lacey, Sidgwick & Jackson
Shanties and Sailors' Songs, Stan Hugill, Jenkins
Shanties from the Seven Seas, Stan Hugill, Routledge and Kegan Paul
Ships and Shipping, M. D. Palmer, Batsford
Some Ship Disasters and Their Causes, K. C. Barnaby, Hutchinson
The Surgeon's Log, J. Johnston Abraham, Penguin
The Sway of the Grand Saloon — a Social History of the North Atlantic, J. M. Brinnin, Macmillan
Transatlantic Paddle Steamers, H. Philip Spratt, Brown, Son & Ferguson
Travelling by Sea in the Nineteenth Century, Basil Greenhill and Ann Giffard, A & C Black

Opposite: conversation on deck.

Index

Illustrations are indicated in bold type